THE BLAME BUSINESS

THE BLAME BUSINESS

THE USES AND MISUSES OF ACCOUNTABILITY

STEPHEN FINEMAN

reaktion books

Published by Reaktion Books Ltd
33 Great Sutton Street
London EC1V 0DX, UK

www.reaktionbooks.co.uk

First published 2015
Copyright © Stephen Fineman 2015

Printed and bound in Great Britain
by Bell & Bain Ltd, Glasgow

A catalogue record for this book is available from the British Library

ISBN 978 1 78023 438 0

Contents

Introduction

Blame is fascinating – it shapes our lives. It can be a benign way of positioning ourselves, a gentle joust or banter, or it can be poisonous, hurtful or devastating for its victims. It can tear apart marriages and fracture work relationships; it can disable major social programmes; it can inflict damage on powerful corporations; it can bring down governments; it can start wars and justify genocides.

Blame is so entrenched in our everyday affairs that it is easy to take for granted, something we just 'do'. Pick up any national newspaper and you will find stories about blame. A twelve-month trawl of the word in the *New York Times* produces some 11,000 hits; we seem obsessed with blame. Indeed, much of our understanding of blame is conditioned by the news – its machinery and its politics. Stirring latent fears and finger-pointing prove to be reliable formulas; blame is what makes and sells news and some exploit this shamelessly.

Blame matters because, seemingly, it explains things: why there is unemployment – 'the government's fault', 'foreigners taking our jobs'; why crime is on the increase – 'incompetent police', 'feral kids'; or why there are more road accidents – 'stupid drivers', 'crazy teenagers'. It is a shortcut to meaning, something to share effortlessly with others. Blame is readily to hand when we feel threatened, hurt or aggrieved. It is patently the language of accusation and self-protection and is often emotional: we blame in exasperation, anger or fury, which rapidly narrows our field of vision.

Why has blame become significant in so many spheres of life? What are its consequences, for good or ill? In exploring these questions I make no pretence to comprehensiveness; this is not a textbook. But I have chosen issues that concern me and that I can examine through the lenses of psychology and sociology.

It would be hard to conceive of a society where blame and righteous anger play no part. Without blame, moral codes, whatever their provenance, would be unenforceable and legal structures unsustainable. If we look at the origins of the term 'blame' it is rooted in ancient ecclesiastical moralizing and disapproval – *blasphemare* – 'speaking evil of'. Blame is therefore a curious paradox: necessary and functional, but also deflective and destructive. It has long defined divisions in society – groups are blamed for who they are or what they represent. In medieval times, witches were singled out; today homosexuals, ethnic minorities, the Roma and asylum seekers can find themselves denounced and excluded. And as the demonization of one group fades, another takes its place. Strip away the prejudices and we typically find the same deep-seated ideologies and anxieties, some nurtured by religious dogma, others reflecting insecurities that a 'proper' way of life is threatened by the presence of 'deviants' or strangers. The 'other' becomes a scapegoat, someone to blame for one's own troubles.

Feeling unjustly blamed can leave its mark, emotional scars that affect behaviour, sometimes for a lifetime – the lot of victims of bullying and harassment. They are vulnerable to online attacks as much as offline abuses of power, all of which raise questions about the perpetrator's make-up and motives. Power abuses permeate blame cultures, organizations that push blame for production problems, errors or faults onto those least able to resist or complain – the junior manager, the field operative. The West Japan Railway Company once demonstrated this tendency. In April 2005 one of its crowded commuter trains derailed at high speed, killing the driver and 106 passengers. A post-mortem of the disaster revealed the fear of blame that dogged the company's drivers. Under pressure of extremely tight schedules, drivers would be blamed for train delays. Penalties on drivers were draconian: they were forced to repent in written reports, verbally abused by their managers and, to compound their humiliation, obliged to undertake menial tasks. Unsurprisingly, they did all they could to cover up any mistakes and were desperate not to be late – on this occasion, too desperate.

There are blamers in society: individuals and organizations intent on holding private and public enterprises to account. They sniff out abuses of privilege and power, corruption and unethical practices. They are a disparate bunch comprising non-governmental organizations, official regulators, inspectorates, shareholders, the press, social media and individual whistle-blowers. Together they represent a remarkable, multi-stranded domain of social conscience, but with widely differing aims and methods, from the aggressively radical to the pedantically bureaucratic. Their most dramatic revelations hit the news – an official caught taking a bribe, the boarding of a vessel fishing illegally, government representatives fiddling their expenses. A high-tide mark was the release by the WikiLeaks organization of thousands of CIA classified documents. They showed the extent of secret state surveillance of its own citizens and other nations' political figures. 'Be accountable!' is the blamer's mantra.

Blamers can face a backlash. Corporations can muster public relations firepower to contest or neutralize them – blaming the blamers. Governments can silence their detractors by isolating or prosecuting them. Public officials and elected politicians are able to create smokescreens of blame avoidance: it was not them but someone else who did it; it was a previous administration; a misunderstanding of the facts; a misreading of the statistics; they were technically within the rules; and so forth. These defensive postures do not always work. The history of whistle-blowing, for example, is dotted with instances where David outflanks Goliath, even if David is bloodied by the encounter. In the 1970s, police officer Frank Serpico of the New York Police Department blew the whistle on corruption and graft in the department. He faced ridicule and reprisals for years at the hands of his superiors and colleagues, but was eventually vindicated by a commission on police corruption. His efforts are credited with changing the culture of the department.

When someone is justly blamed and accepts it, an apology can help – 'a regretful acknowledgement of an offence or failure' in the words of the *Oxford English Dictionary*. The healing powers of apologies are well documented. A well-timed, sincere apology signals a genuine ownership of a problem and a commitment to fix it. Yet, in our individualistic, litigious societies, apologies can come grudgingly, if at all: it is risky and ego-tarnishing to admit one is wrong. Where there is corporate wrongdoing, an apology can spell costly compensation. But there is a fudged alternative – the non-apology. Non-apologies have the appearance of an apology but omit a clear admission of culpability or blame.

Apologies' politics are thorniest when a nation is blamed for its historic abuses or cruelties. Should it, through its current head of state, apologize to victims or their relatives? This delicate territory attracts hawks and doves. Some believe it to be a futile gesture, especially many years after the original event. Others take the opposite view: pain crosses generations and apologizing is a vital step towards repairing the legacy of harm.

Finally, blame and punishment are at the heart of the criminal justice system. The convicted are rarely expected to put things right with their victims – serving their sentence fulfils their obligation to society. In the eyes of critics this amounts to justice half-done because it marginalizes the victims. Beyond the occasional victim statement read out in court, the needs, traumas, fears and losses of victims are largely ignored. Restorative justice is one response to this. It does not let the convicted offender off the hook, but enables both parties to meet and try to forge a mutual understanding. There is space for remorse from the perpetrator and forgiveness from the victim. Restorative justice has been applied to schools, workplaces and nations, at times demonstrating that blame need not be a cul-de-sac for anger and resentment.

In the pages to follow I say more about these matters and the dilemmas they pose. Blame may not explain all the evils of the world, but it sometimes gets pretty close.

1

Why Do We Blame?

The date was 29 February 1692; the place, Salem, Massachusetts. The two children Elizabeth Parris and Abigail Williams could have had little idea of the furore they were about to unleash. Under the steely gaze of local magistrates the children nervously pointed the finger at three women: elderly and impoverished Sarah Osborne; Tituba, a slave worker employed by Elizabeth's Puritan father, Pastor Samuel Parris; and Sarah Good, a homeless beggar. Indoctrinated to fear witches, the girls said that the women were to blame for their fits – screaming, contortions and unpredictable behaviour – today put down to ergot, a cereal fungus.

Blaming witches for misfortunes already had a long history, embedded in religious superstitions across Europe. Between 1300 and 1600 many thousands of women were accused of witchcraft and being in league with the Devil, often on the flimsiest of pretexts. Actual trials were relatively rare, but punishment befell about half the accused, often torture and death – a draconian fate for what is now an imaginary crime. In Britain, James VI of Scotland, who became James I of England, added his own authority to the witch frenzy with his book *Daemonologie*. He was convinced that witches were a malign influence in his kingdom and also responsible for his own close encounters with death.

In Salem local circumstances shaped the fervour. A beleaguered Reverend Parris preached provocative sermons which did not go down well with many of his parishioners; he was fast losing moral authority. Prominent church members feared their church was seriously under attack. To Reverend Parris this was all the work of the Devil. Meanwhile, the local community was facing the threat of war, disease and poverty, further fuelling fear. All these conditions lent themselves to scapegoating: someone had to be blamed and witches fitted the bill. Tituba's confession sealed the women's fate. She captivated magistrates with her tales of witches flying on poles, and magic rituals to alleviate the girls' suffering. The women were convicted of witchcraft and incarcerated in a local jail. Witch fever and paranoia continued in the region for about a year and a half, culminating in some 1,600 suspects and twenty executions.

It would be comforting to think that the belief in witches and their malevolent power is now a historical curiosity, a quirk of irrational pre-Enlightenment times, but this would be wrong. In the unsettling words of the United Nations Human Rights Council, 'The age-old belief in the power of witchcraft is still widely held throughout Africa . . . causing great suffering to innocent people.'[1] It is also present in Papua New Guinea, Saudi Arabia, India and parts of Europe. Witchcraft is blamed for all manner of troubles, from death and disease to accidents and business failure. Many of India's poor rural communities are steeped in magic and mysticism, and personal adversity is put down to witchcraft. In 2011, for example, a family in Chhattisgarh, central India, blamed a neighbour for causing their money troubles and poor health. Eleven people stormed her house accusing her of witchcraft, blinding her and her husband by stabbing them in the eyes with scissors.[2] On other occasions women accused of witchcraft have been paraded naked or killed. The tribal areas of India are rarely impacted by the law, so these events often go unreported.

The fear of witchcraft has been profitable for so-called pastor prophets, a social elite in parts of Africa, some of whom are conspicuous for their wealth and personal media channels. They claim to be able to identify 'the possessed' and to 'spiritually heal' them – for a fee. In her book *Unveiling the Mysteries of Witchcraft*, Pastor Helen Ukpabio explains that 'if a child under the age of two screams in the night, cries and is always feverish with deteriorating health, he or she is a servant of Satan.'[3] Her recommended treatment varies, but includes 'curative' oils and potions, beatings, injecting petrol in the eyes or ears, forced fasting and isolation.

Witch persecution in Europe is an under-the-radar crime. In the UK between 2002 and 2012 there were 83 investigations into faith-based child abuse, and some were linked to witchcraft, such as the fate of fifteen-year-old Kristy Bamu. He was visiting the UK with four of his sisters, staying with his eldest sister and her Congolese boyfriend in their London apartment. The couple were immersed in witchcraft and were convinced that their visitors were bent on bringing evil into their home and had come to kill them. The children were viciously attacked. Only when Kristy's younger sisters 'confessed' to being witches did they escape further assault. Kristy was less fortunate; he died of his injuries.[4]

Myths, superstitions and fears are at the root of witch folklore. But we no longer need to believe in 'actual' witches to have witch-hunts – any person or group that appears to cause us problems can be witch-hunted if we can convince ourselves and others that there is sufficient reason. Ideological threat is one excuse – such as 1950s McCarthyism aimed at 'un-Americans' in the U.S., and the 'contaminative influence' of Jews and homosexuals on the Nazis. A group's economic success in a poor or troubled country can mark it out for blame and persecution, for instance the fate of the Tutsis in Rwanda and the Asians in Uganda. The Ugandan witch-hunt was orchestrated by its president, Idi Amin, who, capitalizing on a long history of Indophobia, proclaimed that God had instructed him to expel all Asians who were 'exploiting' the local economy. It created a frantic exodus of some 50,000 people.

Given the frequent re-emergence of witch-hunts, it is unsurprising that survivors of persecution never entirely relax. When will I be singled out again because of my religion, sexuality, colour – or something else?

Scapegoats and Stigma

Scapegoating is central to witch-hunts and has long played a role in the way a society defends itself from its anxieties and threats. By scapegoating, people free themselves of culpability, shifting blame onto an innocent target, be it a person or a group. In the words of anthropologist James George Frazer, it is 'a palming off upon someone else the trouble which a man shrinks from bearing himself'.[5] Nations palm off their troubles on other nations, management on unions, unions on management, family members on one another. Feuding parents scapegoat their children for their own shortcomings; teenagers incriminate weaker members of their peer group for their own faults; executives accuse junior staff rather than taking the blame for their own misjudgements. Governments create scapegoats to deflect public attention from their policy defects or mistakes.

In biblical times a scapegoat was literally a goat. There was a belief that sin and ill-fortune were transferable between beings, so on the important Day of Atonement a goat would carry Israel's guilt into the wilderness. It was expected to perish during its wanderings and thus cleanse the Children of Israel of their sins – for another year at any rate. The scapegoat ritual in ancient Greece (*pharmakos*) was also a purification, but via a human carrier. During periods of pestilence, famine, blight or plague, someone was drawn from the margins of society to be scapegoat – a low-class person, a criminal or a person who happened to be very ugly. The ritual was so vital to the community that the victim was carefully cosseted and fed on foods of special purity for a year before they were cast out. Then, elaborately robed, they were led through the streets to be roundly abused and finally ejected from the city. This custom was not fixed in form. One variation subjected the unfortunate male victim to a flogging seven times on his penis with wild fig branches. He was then burnt on a pyre of wood from wild trees, and finally his ashes were scattered into the sea to purify the city of its ills.[6]

Scapegoating people who are physically strange or different is a recurring, primitive, social impulse. Psychologist Betty Adelson recounts the Inca practice of using dwarfs as scapegoats. She tells of the fate of a dwarf captured by one of the last Inca rulers. On the occasion of the ruler's death the dwarf was attacked by members of the grieving funeral cortège for the injustice of the loss of their 'wonderful ruler' and being left with a 'miserable and luckless wretch who had not enjoyed the luck of being a man'.[7] Today, in parts of East Africa, children and adults with albinism, a rare genetic defect that produces skin, eyes and hair with no colour, are cursed and ostracized as bringers of bad luck. The power of physical revulsion has not been lost on propagandists of scapegoating. During the Rwanda genocide, government broadcasts likened the Tutsis to 'cockroaches' to be exterminated, and the Nazis produced ugly portraits of Jews in their anti-Semitic cartoons and posters.

The Scapegoat in the Workplace

It took me about two years of frustration, anger, depression, physical exhaustion, utter detachment, fatigue and sleeplessness, to realize that I have become a 'target', a 'scapegoat' for the office dysfunction. Beginning with the Director all the way down to the mail clerk. Upon further research I realized that what I thought was only my imagination, turned out to be reality, and that others suffer the same type of silent torture, endured daily, with no one to discuss this with, especially their direct superior, because the supervisor wittingly or unwittingly condones this type of behavior. I tried appealing to my Director on an emotional level, an intellectual level, a professional level, and worst of all, a personal level, that was my second mistake.[8]

Victimization and scapegoating in the workplace is an enduring phenomenon. It is estimated to affect over twelve million workers across Europe and over a third of the U.S. workforce. It is a grown-up version of what happens in the school playground: picking on vulnerable or 'different' individuals and harassing or bullying them, often relentlessly.[9] Workplace bullies now also enjoy the anonymity and disinhibition of the Internet to post demeaning or threatening messages. An Australian study reports some one in ten workers are cyber-bullied in this way, many exposed to twin-prong attacks – online and face to face.[10] The victims often serve as innocent targets for an individual or work group's frustrations and, as in the case above, feel intimidated and trapped – worn down, unable to fight back.

The abuse of power, explicitly in the formal hierarchy or implicitly within the work group, lies at the heart of bullying and harassment. In sexual harassment women are exposed to a double jeopardy: gender stereotyping and marginalization. They are, in effect, punished if they fail to live up to the feminine ideal as defined by sexist males and the norms of 'boys' clubs' at work. Women who reach top positions typically have to prove themselves against male rules and tolerate a degree of sexual harassment to survive.[11] Their increased formal power in the workplace provides no foolproof protection, and many report feeling isolated.

It is a truism that harassment and bullying often tell us more about the perpetrator than the victim. Indeed, when there are no obvious differences that mark out potential victims, a bully can invent some for their own purposes. Bullies' actions are often traceable to their own past troubles, many having been bullied themselves. They act out their difficulties by diminishing others. They can appear narcissistic, emotionally cold, unable to empathize with others. Few bullies admit that what they do is bullying, but will rationalize their actions: their victim was to blame, 'they asked for it'. Psychoanalyst Carl Jung interpreted this as an extreme version of tendencies that we all carry – a deeply rooted urge to blame others. It is self-protective; it makes us feel better because we do not have to admit personal responsibility. Jung proposed a shadow side to our character where the faults, weaknesses, insecurities, aggressions, hates and sexual impulses reside, but pushed out of our consciousness. Yet they continue to shape our behaviour in the self-righteous condemnation of others for the faults we cannot admit in ourselves.

Externalizing our frustrations and shortcomings in this manner is a kind of psychological dumping: it elevates our own status by diminishing others, and after discharging our burden we feel more at ease – for a while. Jung argued that the shadow operates at both an individual and collective level. In the latter, a group or population projects its collective shadow – economic failure, prejudices, biases, fears – onto a convenient scapegoat such as another nation or community. Jung was gloomy in his prognostications: there is no escape from the shadow; it cannot be willed away. New targets – people to blame, scapegoats – are created as old ones disappear. A 'happy tribe' is bought at the cost of the victim's misery.[12]

Culturally entrenched bullying is self-sealing. In workplaces where stress levels are high and/or a macho culture is prized, it can be accepted sanguinely: 'it's not really bullying'; 'it's the way people are around here'; it 'helps toughen us up'. Victims will often feel trapped in a code of silence that can only be broken by public exposure – a major crisis, a whistle-blower, media exposé, the intervention of an official regular. Anti-bullying policies are now common to many organizations, but they mean little unless they are part of the working culture. This normally means strong, zero-tolerance leadership, safe support for victims and effective penalties for perpetrators.

The Stigmatized

Stigmas define the lowest order of social prestige, originating in the ancient Greek practice of physically branding with a burn or scar those considered the dregs of society – the traitors, the criminals, the slaves. It was a permanently visible sign of inferior status and social exclusion. The technique was chillingly reproduced some 2,000 years later in the tattooed numbers on Nazi concentration camp victims, but the Nazis added their own embellishments – compulsory badges of shame produced on an industrial scale. The yellow, star-shaped 'race defiler' badge is commonly cited, but there were many others of different colours and shapes: a red triangle for political enemies, a green triangle for professional criminals, a brown triangle for Gypsies, a pink triangle for homosexuals and a purple triangle for Jehovah's Witnesses.

There are people whose physical or psychological condition is their stigma, defined 'as' or by their condition: 'a paraplegic', 'a depressive', 'a schizophrenic'. Their disability or difference socially marginalizes them, something they cannot remove or wish away. Other stigmas single out the 'morally inferior': the criminal, the prostitute, the Dalits of India, homosexuals in many parts of Africa. Precisely who is stigmatized speaks of the mores of the time and the influence of moral gatekeepers, religious and civil. The story of single motherhood is an illuminating example.

Single mothers have long been relegated to the margins of society, stigmatized and scapegoated for their 'moral decline'. In England their inferior status was officially underlined by the Poor Law of 1834. They were charged with full responsibility for their offspring and denied any assistance for their 'bastard' children, while the father was let off scot-free. A condemnatory Church added to their misery – they were sinful, fallen women.

Accounts of unmarried mothers of the era make uncomfortable reading. In disgrace, a pregnant young woman would be forced out of her family. Some committed infanticide or turned in desperation to the shadowy services of baby farmers. Dorothy Haller, in 'Bastardy and Baby Farming in Victorian England', chronicles the practice. Baby farmers treated unwanted infants as commodities. For a set fee they would adopt the baby but dispose of it as soon as possible. Infants 'were kept drugged on laudanum, paregoric, and other poisons, and fed watered down milk'. Sick infants were a better buy 'because life was precarious for them and their deaths would appear more natural'. Haller cites the example of baby farmer Charlotte Winsor:

> On February 15, 1865, the body of Mary Jane Harris' four-month-old son was found wrapped up in a copy of the *Western Times* beside a road in Torquay. Miss Harris had farmed out the child to Mrs Winsor for 3s a week, and, at first, resisted Mrs Winsor's offer to dispose of the child. When the burden of its support became too much she stood by and watched Charlotte Winsor smother her son and wrap his naked body in an old newspaper; the body was later dumped on the roadside.[13]

There were institutions where unmarried mothers could hide their shame, or be forcefully hidden away. Some mothers were prostitutes, ostracized by the Victorian middle and upper classes, not without a whiff of hypocrisy: premarital sex for middle- and upper-class men was mostly with prostitutes and servants. Convent organizations played a major role, especially the Catholic Magdalene Asylums of North America, Europe, Britain and Ireland. In the Republic of Ireland they became known as Magdalene Laundries, which were notionally rehabilitative but in practice more like prisons where young pregnant girls were sent to work in sweatshop conditions. A typical schedule was a ten-hour day for six days a week, silence imposed. Laundry work dominated their life, the hard labour of removing stains from clothing intended as a cleansing of the soul as much as the garments.

Babies could be delivered in the institution but were promptly taken by the nuns to be placed in orphanages, or handed over to wealthy couples seeking a child in return for a 'donation'. The laundries were profitable, principally because the workers received no pay. Some 10,000 women passed through them in the nineteenth century. Many spent the rest of their lives there to be interred in the convent's grounds or in mass burial plots. The last Magdalene Laundry survived well into the twentieth century.

On the other side of the globe, in Australia, unmarried mothers faced similar conservative values. In the 1950s and '60s they were encouraged to think of themselves as unfit for motherhood and were pressed to give up their babies. There was also a belief that the nation's virtue depended upon the success of the white, nuclear family, so some 150,000 white babies were sent out for adoption. The policy was underwritten by influential psychologists of the time who regarded the mothers as essentially unstable characters and unfit for motherhood, but their newborns were 'blank slates' and easily transferrable into the bosom of a 'secure family'.[14] The legacy for many mothers was traumatic:

> My mother became hysterical, when she realized I was pregnant, she was bereft about the neighbours, the relatives, and the church members, finding out her daughter was pregnant out-of wedlock . . . I had to hide in the house, she had contempt for me . . . It was decided that I go to a home for unmarried mothers 'for a few weeks' so I would not been [sic] seen by others who would make judgement.

• • •

> [My father] took me to Windang police station and told them what was going on. I think he was hoping I would tell them who the father was. In those days carnal knowledge was a crime. My father got angrier and angrier; he punched me in the face in front of the police, who did nothing. About an hour later a lady came to the police station and took me home and told me to pack a bag.

• • •

A mother whose child has been stolen does not only remember in her mind, she remembers with every fibre of her being.[15]

Nowadays lone mothers have become a familiar addition to non-traditional forms of family, yet population surveys continue to tap a vein of prejudice: many people see single mothers as not entirely respectable. In the UK single mothers rank low on the list of those judged most deserving of state support, especially if they are unwilling to seek work when their children reach school age.[16] Conservative values readily surface across the major religions.[17] Evangelical Christians are disapproving and deny single mothers any assistance. Orthodox Jews take a dim view of single motherhood, which they see as a threat to the sanctity of the family. The Islamist position is similar, but its hardliners go further by denying single mothers a place in an Islamist state.[18] India's widespread intolerance of single mothers can be traced to the Hindu belief that single parenting is a violation of the purity of family and marriage.[19]

Single mothers fare best in liberal, secularized societies such as Denmark, Sweden and Germany. These countries try to balance the child's needs with those of the parent, be it a one- or two-parent family, with or without a male head.

Skewed Judgements

Attributing our failures to external causes (you, them, bad weather, bad luck, poor equipment, unfair rules) and successes to internal causes (my skill, my abilities, my personality) are some of the oldest phenomena to be studied by social psychologists. In the 1950s, Austrian psychologist Fritz Heider drew attention to the 'fundamental attribution errors' we make about causality because we unconsciously adjust our perceptions to protect our self-esteem, values and prejudices.[20] Accordingly we often blame with two voices: one when we are the perpetrator and play down the repercussions on our victim; the other when we are the victim and complain of long-lasting personal offence.[21] There is a clue here as to why some international grievances fester for generations, such as Arab tribulations over the Crusades, bitterness of Palestinians towards Israeli annexation of their land, and continuing resentment about the American Civil War in the Southern states.

The attribution biases permeate blame situations, such as blaming rape victims for 'bringing it on themselves'. Some of its nuances were explored by researchers Amy Grubb and Julie Harrower of Coventry University.[22] After showing a large group of men and women different rape scenarios, they found that men were more likely to blame the victim than women (a cautionary note for male-led justice systems and juror selection), and that victims who had initially agreed to engage with the person who attacked them – meeting in a bar, a date – were judged as more personally to blame for their predicament. These biases sit uneasily with the ideal that no woman should ever be blamed for her own rape and the power abuses that cause it.

To Blame, to Praise

Blame and praise were probably useful to our hominid ancestors some 2.6 million years ago. Charles Darwin concluded that fear of blame and love of praise were crucial to the cooperative behaviour that helped the survival of a social unit. By their capacity to imitate, early humans learned that helping others could be rewarded by receiving help in return, and 'from this low motive', wrote Darwin, 'he might acquire the habit of aiding his fellows; and the habit of performing benevolent actions certainly strengthens feelings of sympathy which gives first impulse to benevolent actions'.[23]

Yet in modern life there is an asymmetry between the praise and blame; our narratives of blame are generally more expansive than that of praise. For instance, we condemn people who commit crimes, but rarely praise those who do not; we censure bad or reckless drivers, but do not heap accolades on the many people who drive safely; we freely scorn the sexually promiscuous, yet praise for the sexually temperate is muted. Praise often takes the backstage. Its social consequences appear less salient, less to do with big issues such as safety, liberty or moral propriety.

The blame/praise calculus reflects what society values as praiseworthy or not, but the tilt to the negative means that others' failures are more likely to be recalled than their successes. Political reputations and business careers are shaped in this way. Howard Raines, for example, was executive editor of the *New York Times* between 2001 and 2003, during which his company earned the accolade of seven Pulitzer prizes for the important stories it published. However, it was his autocratic style that was most remembered and was eventually to unseat him. It was alleged that he was callous, dividing his staff into 'also-rans' and 'stars', creating disarray and disaffection.[24] Another example is the late Leona Helmsley, leader of a hotel chain in the 1980s. She was known as a perfectionist who expected perfection from her staff – a tough style that resulted in a very successful business. Nevertheless, her way of operating eventually proved toxic for the organization. She was dubbed 'the Queen of Mean' by the tabloid press and internal whistle-blowers raised questions over her tax affairs, for which she was prosecuted. In her trial an employee reported her as saying that 'only the little people pay taxes', a tag she would never be able to shake off.[25]

However, the negative 'rule' is not altogether straightforward. History can be rewritten to mask the negative, or transform the blameworthy into praiseworthy. There are ruthless political leaders now glorified by the very people who once suffered at their hands: nearly half of Russians hold a positive view of Stalin, while Chairman Mao's despotic legacy is dwarfed by his positive image as a modernizer of China and symbol of communistic values.[26] Great artistic achievement can determine a person's reputation, eclipsing faults or misdeeds in other spheres of their life. Wagner remains a much a lauded composer despite his well-known anti-Semitism, and Picasso's celebrated status has not been noticeably dented by the misery he is said to have brought to the many women in his life. One, Dora Maar, described him as an extraordinary artist, but 'morally speaking worthless'.[27] Lawbreakers too can be glamorized and elevated to folk heroes: Ned Kelly, Robin Hood, the Great Train Robbers and Bonnie and Clyde. Praise, like blame, is a somewhat malleable social commodity.

Bystanders and Blame

Nottingham, England, 2010. It was 3 a.m. and one of the coldest nights of the year. A 22-year-old law student boarded the night bus home after a festive night out. The bus was buzzing with revellers. She started to pay the driver for a £5 ticket, but found that she was just 20 pence short. She asked the driver if he could wait while she visited a cash machine. He refused. She asked if she could pay next time. He refused. Increasingly anxious, she asked if she could pay at the destination stop where her mother would be waiting. He refused. CCTV footage captured her looking pleadingly at the dozens of passengers on the bus and those pushing past her. No one offered help and she was ejected from the bus. On her long walk home she was grabbed by a man, dragged into a recreation ground and viciously raped, so brutally that she was not recognized by her mother who had been desperately searching for her.

The bus driver's bureaucratic insensitivity was a clear link in the tragic chain of events, but what of the many passengers on the bus? Surely someone could have stepped forward to give the student a mere 20 pence? They were demonstrating the remarkably pervasive bystander effect – witnessing suffering but doing nothing about it. The very presence of other people increases the inhibition to help, as does a belief that the victim probably brought the problem on themselves. Some bystanders say that they feel guilty after such incidents and wish they could have handled things differently, but during the event they somehow felt incapable.

The bystander effect is pervasive; we are all potential bystanders. It is, explain psychologists, the result of a diffusion of responsibility: 'Someone else is probably going to intervene, so why should I?' People typically scan the faces in the crowd to pick up cues about what others are thinking. As most of them are doing what bystanders do – nothing – it is taken as a further justification not to get involved. In the bustle of crowds we are less likely to notice someone in trouble, or interpret an event as urgent; we walk on by.

Bystanding is not confined to one-off incidents: whole populations stand by while others suffer or are persecuted. There is a collective diffusion of responsibility that leaves even the best-intentioned incapable of responding. In an elegy attributed to pacifist pastor Martin Niemöller, the moral failure of the German people to speak out against the Nazis, including himself, is lamented:

> First they came for the Socialists, and I did not speak out – Because I was not a Socialist.
> Then they came for the Trade Unionists, and I did not speak out – Because I was not a Trade Unionist.
> Then they came for the Jews, and I did not speak out – Because I was not a Jew.
> Then they came for me – and there was no one left to speak for me.[28]

Victoria Barnett, in her book *Bystanders: Conscience and Complicity During the Holocaust*, echoes Niemöller's sentiments, evoking the banality of Germany's collective deafness and blindness:

> In some fashion these people simply went about their daily lives during one of the ghastliest dictatorships the world has

ever known. They continued to work and raise their children. Those who lived near concentration camps tended their gardens and had regular dealings with those who worked and ran the camps. After November 9, 1938, when thousands of Jewish-owned businesses in Germany suddenly had new owners, people continued to shop in them as though nothing had changed.[29]

In many respects it was in German citizens' interests not to want to know the full extent of what was happening. Most of them were experiencing the social and economic difficulties that the Nazis promised to alleviate – which they did. The unemployment rate fell and there was a new sense of camaraderie and optimism. Gratitude to Hitler merged with his hatred of the Jews; it was all part of the package. The Jews became an acceptable population to persecute and blame. Ask no questions and suppress any concerns.

It was a shrill awakening when the German people were compelled to confront the full implications of what they had signed up to, as the events of 18 April 1945 testify. On that day 1,200 citizens of Weimar, a city just four miles away from the Buchenwald concentration camp, were brought to the camp to see the horror perpetrated in their name. A *New York Times* reporter was there to describe the scene:

> One of the first things that the German civilian visitors saw as they passed through the gates and into the interior was a display of 'parchment'. This consisted of large pieces of human flesh on which were elaborate tattooed markings [and] two large table lamps with parchment shade also made of human flesh . . . The German people saw all this today, and they wept. Those who didn't weep said they were ashamed. They said they didn't know about it.
>
> There were human skeletons who had lost all likeness to anything human . . . They were dying and no one could do

anything about it. Some Germans were sceptical at first as if this show had been staged for their benefit, but they were soon convinced . . . Men went white and women turned away. It was too much for them.[30]

Today population bystanding continues, although public ignorance about what is going on in one's own, or another's, backyard, is much rarer thanks to the Internet and international news channels. Horrors on the screen are startling, yet can soon appear distant and fragmentary: we disengage; it is other people's business. Our political leaders are informed by sophisticated surveillance techniques, including real-time images of human suffering and persecution, yet they, too, can seem unable or unwilling to act. Behind their inertia is a bigger game of political alliances and national self-interest. Another country's persecutions or abuse of human rights are of 'extreme concern' – the closest statement to blame – but a nation rarely sees itself as responsible for those beyond its borders, until, that is, its strategic (political or commercial) interests are seriously threatened. Intergovernmental organizations and NGOs are there to challenge passive bystanding, and have achieved some significant successes, such as in Cambodia, El Salvador, Mozambique, Sierra Leone, Burundi and Kosovo. But there is also a trail of failures, victims of schisms between core members of the organizations.

Bystanding in the street, the school playground or the workplace has attracted the attention of educators and trainers. One school programme emphasizes the inappropriateness of witnessing other children bullying and doing nothing about it: how would they feel if they were being victimized and no one helped them? The victim does not deserve it because they are 'weak'; it is an emergency event, not 'fun', and there are safe ways to intervene or to seek help.[31]

Workplace anti-bullying training employs scenarios and role playing that simulate bystanding, followed by discussions on how 'active' bystanding can be encouraged.[32] On occasion a crisis forces some organizations to adopt these measures, the position of California's Department of Justice in the 1990s. It followed the savage beating of black detainee Rodney King by police, which was caught on tape and broadcast worldwide. The department consulted a psychology professor to advise them on how to prevent such an event happening again. 'The police have a conception', observed the professor, 'as part of their culture that the way you police a fellow officer is to support what they're doing and that can lead to tragedy, both for the citizens and the police.' In training sessions he challenged this local wisdom and taught officers how they could intervene early enough before a fellow officer resorted to excessive force, and thus avoid the trap of becoming a bystander.[33]

Blame, Shame and Honour

Looting and arson afflicted London and other UK cities in the summer of 2011. 'The people who wrecked swathes of property, burned vehicles and terrorized communities have no moral compass to make them susceptible to guilt or shame', observed Max Hastings of the *Daily Mail*. He continued: 'Most have no jobs to go to or exams they might pass. They know no family role models, for most live in homes in which the father is unemployed, or from which he has decamped.'[34]

The journalist was making a political point, but in doing so touched on some psychological truths: shame and guilt are not mere augmentations to blame, they are central to it, and they are learned. The anticipation of these feelings is a self-policing mechanism and is the basis of our mutual understandings and moral orders. When they are absent or fail to function, much social control is lost. Shame, especially, is one of our master emotions, intrinsic to successful socialization; an internalized image of cultural values and demands. As Samuel Johnson reflected, 'Where there is yet shame, there may in time be virtue.'[35]

Shaming routines and rituals have long played a role in the assignment of blame, reminding others what is in store for them should they stray from the straight and narrow. Their role was well understood by our medieval forebears who installed stocks and pillories on their village greens for the public humiliation of minor offenders. Their importance was enshrined in statute in Tudor England, with prescribed time-tariffs for different mis-demeanours: one hour for swearing, four hours for being drunk and up to three days for vagabonding (regarded as a particular threat to civil order). Other shamings of the time were more parochial, such as the folk custom of charivari. Villagers would take up their fifes, horns, pots and pans, and make 'rough music' outside the dwellings of moral offenders. It created a cacophony that would draw public attention to the unfortunate miscre-ant – an adulterer, a wife beater, an unmarried mother, a remarried widow or widower.

In the nineteenth century the shaming practice of cashiering evolved to punish military officers found guilty of major rule-breaking. The cashiering of Alfred Dreyfus, a Jewish captain in the French army, stands as a notorious example. He was convicted of high treason for passing secret information to the German enemy. On 5 January 1895, before an assembled regiment, his stripes were ceremonially torn off and his sword broken. Then 'in torment and agony' and protesting his inno-cence, he was ushered through a baying crowd to a police wagon, and onward to Devil's Island penal colony to begin a life sentence. It took another eleven years before it was formally acknowledged that the wrong man had been convicted and that rampant anti-Semitism within the French army had led to a cover-up. Cashiering remains a punishment for senior military officers who breach military discipline, but now without the ostentatious trappings.

Today, stocks, pillories and the like are museum pieces, but shaming practices and rituals remain. Street gatherings and marches ridicule and humiliate unpopular leaders and politicians. Edgy comedians, cartoonists and playwrights lampoon the hypocrisies of public figures. There are league tables that name and shame institutions and corporations for their poor performance or mal-practice. Social media circulate exposés of 'shameful' lives and, like the pillories of old, invite others to cast their own stones, but now in web comments and tweets.

Honour

Honour cultures are defined by shame and blame. A slight in honour culture questions the recipient's integrity and reputation and demands a counter-attack; not to do so deepens shame and status loss. Historically, honour has been an extraordinarily potent force – something to seek, defend, fight over or die for.

Honour initially evolved as an important protocol among tribal, tight-knit groups of kin. Protection from the state was weak or absent so codes of honour – conveyed in stories, customs, brave acts and sacrifices – determined what was right and proper for members of the group. Man's quest for honour can be found in the ancient Greek *Iliad*, in the poems of Homer and the plays of Shakespeare ('Life every man holds dear, but the dear man holds honour far more precious dear than life': *Troilus and Cressida*, v:iii, 33–4). The signatories to the u.s. Declaration of Independence pledged their 'sacred honor' to each other and, up until the 1960s, to honour – and obey – was a common wifely vow in the marriage ceremony. Anthropologists regard honour as two-dimensional. There is horizontal honour – the right to be respected by one's equals, wholly dependent on meeting strict standards approved by the group. And there is vertical honour – special privileges (praise, respect, rank) to those who do particularly well on the horizontal criteria.[36]

Traditional cultures around the Mediterranean region have long prized the honour of the family.[37] Men have been charged with protecting family honour by demonstrating toughness, while sexual shame and chastity have been central to a woman's honour or dishonour. Speedy retribution salvages pride and honour – for a time. Some blood feuds and family vendettas cross the generations, in Corsica, for example, well into the twentieth century. One estimate is that, from a population of 120,000, some 30,000 Corsicans lost their lives to vendettas between 1683 and 1715.[38]

Family honour continues to define the moral order in parts of Central Asia and East Africa, a cultural practice often attached to Islamic beliefs and prohibitions. It can spell harsh justice for a young Muslim woman who brings shame on her family by refusing an arranged marriage, fleeing an abusive marriage, having pre-marital sex, being raped (resulting in her being 'impure') or being 'too Western'. According to the United Nations there are some 5,000 so-called honour killings each year, some among Asian immigrant families in the West.[39] The Shafia family in Canada was one of them. The affront to Mohammad Shafia's authority and honour was too much when his two eldest daughters wanted boyfriends in defiance of his wishes, and his wife sought to escape her loveless marriage to him. In 2012 he arranged their killings, and that of a younger daughter, faking an accident that submerged their car in a lock and drowned them. The case jolted the Islamic Supreme Council of Canada into signing a fatwa to counter misinterpretations of the Quran, ruling that honour killings, domestic violence and misogyny played no part in Islam.

Modern societies have substituted honour codes with systems of ethics and third party justice – police, courts of law and institutionalized punishment. However, vestiges of traditional honour can still be found among gangs, sports teams and the military. Honour symbols persist, such as ceremonies and medals that celebrate courage and daring. Vertical honour is preserved in deferential modes of address – 'your honour' to judges, the 'right honourable' to members of parliament in the UK. It is now rare in advanced democracies for people to take deep umbrage over honour impugned, although James Bowman, author of

Honor: A History, invites us to test this out by calling a man a wimp and a woman a slut: 'These are still fighting words,' he submits, 'though less likely to accrue mortal consequences than in the days when they or their equivalents would have required men to shoot at each other.'[40]

Fragmenting Blame

Much has been written about the shift in the West from traditional, absolute values to fragmentation – the postmodern, 'me' society. A recent U.S. study exposes some of its features. It quizzed young adults about what they saw as today's moral dilemmas, but many were confused by the question. Right and wrong in this form rarely figured in the way they saw the world; it was more a relaxed individualism, as one respondent explained:

> I think morals are entirely made up. I don't believe in rules or law. I think things like scientific laws are the only things that we notice to be true in most instances. So nothing, I don't believe that anything can ever be 100 percent true.[41]

As old verities begin to be doubted, so does the meaning of what is blameworthy and shameworthy – the cause of much hand-wringing among traditional moral guardians. Fearing chaos, Christian fundamentalists have likened the moral slippage to a disease that can only be cured by a return to the 'word of God'. Liberal Christianity, on the other hand, has chosen not to dig trenches while the tide is coming in and has tried to engage with the changing social climate and new pluralism.

All morals are fashioned from competing ideologies, superstitions and religious claims. The fact that nowadays young people are less able or willing to reproduce 'foundational' moral certainties, virtues and vices, should not mean that they cannot function fairly and humanely. And if evolutionists are correct, there will always be the pull towards reciprocity – doing some things for each other. The reactionary voices of a new generation add, as they always have done, to the dynamism and tensions of moral debates. Blame is liberated from some of its old prisons, but perhaps to enter new ones.

2
Panics Old and New

It was Easter 1964 in Clacton, a modest holiday resort on the English coast. The weather was doing its worst, wet and cold; trade was sluggish and

> the young people had their own boredom and irritation fanned by rumour of café owners and barmen refusing to serve some of them. A few groups started scuffling on the pavement and throwing stones at each other. The Mods and Rockers factions – a division initially based on clothes and life styles, later rigidified, but at that time not fully established – started separating out. Those on bikes and scooters roared up and down, windows were broken, some beach huts were wrecked and one boy fired a starting pistol in the air. The vast number of people crowding into the street, the noise, everyone's general irritation and actions of an unprepared and undermanned police force had the effect of making the two days unpleasant, oppressive and sometimes frightening.

This is Stanley Cohen's description of what happened on that day.[1] Cohen, a sociologist, was curious about how the press reported it. The story was carried in every national paper and the overseas press. The headlines were of shock and horror: 'Day of Terror by Scooter Groups', 'Youngsters Beat Up Town – 97 Leather Jacket Arrests', 'Wild Ones Invade Seaside', and 'West Side Story on the English Coast'. In Cohen's eyes all this appeared a striking exaggeration of what actually went on. A moral panic was being constructed: moral in the condemnation of the people involved, panic in the hysteria of the reaction. Mods and Rockers were, in Cohen's terms, cast as folk devils, deviant outsiders to whom all manner of misdemeanours could be attributed. They joined the ranks of 1960s Teddy Boys, Hell's Angels and skinheads. For Cohen the major problem was one of disproportionality: the moral panic was way out of kilter with the moral threat. The Mods and Rockers in Clacton were a post-war, post-military-service generation, expressing new identities and freedom on a holiday weekend – a lean time for the news. There was little animosity between the groups at this juncture, no pitched battles, and the actual damage caused amounted to £513, a small sum even by the standards of the day. They were demonized by the media and punished by an outraged and baffled establishment.

Folk devilling is all-encompassing and leaves little room for doubt about the threat: 'bankers are greedy parasites'; 'pro-abortionists are murderers'; 'Gypsies are filthy thieves', and so forth. Stereotyping and naive labelling bunches many different people into single categories that are easy to grasp; it avoids the exceptions or deeper explanations: 'they' are the problem; 'they' are to blame. Some of 'them' live in separate communities or on the edge of society and make easy targets, such as ethnic and religious minorities, new immigrants or youth gangs.

Each era creates its folk devils, something or someone to blame for threatening its way of life, a category that slips easily into common vernacular. In eighteenth-century England it was 'marauding' thieves and thugs from the 'criminal classes', a major worry to their more privileged superiors. In the early nineteenth century it was the 'Yellow Peril', Chinese immigrant labourers who were seen as a threat to local jobs and the 'civilized' West, not dissimilar to today's perceptions of migrants from Eastern Europe and the African continent. These fears and attributions may be real in the eye of the beholder, but the hard facts rarely bear out the level of concern. Historian Robert Hughes puts it down to the 'tyranny of moral generalization over social inspection'.[2]

Spreading the (Bad) News

On 17 July 1862 Hugh Pilkington, member of parliament, was on his way home after a late sitting at the House of Commons. He was set upon, choked and robbed of his gold watch. The choking or strangling of victims – garrotting, as it was called at the time – was nothing new to Victorian London, as historical letters to *The Times* attest:

> On Saturday, the 1st inst., when returning home at night, and as usual walking quick, I was, without any warning, suddenly seized from behind by some one, who, placing the bend of his arm to my throat, and then clasping his right wrist with his left-hand, thereby forming a powerful lever, succeeded in effectually strangling me for a time, and rendering me incapable of moving or even calling for assistance, although there was plenty at hand, whilst a second easily rifled me of all he could find (12 February 1851).

But it was Hugh Pilkington's plight that instigated press frenzy about a vile breed of criminal who stalked the streets of Victorian London, who would stop at nothing to get what he wanted. A moral panic was created. The police and magistrates began redefining minor crimes, such as pickpocketing, as garrotting. It instantly inflated the statistics on violent crime, which in turn fuelled the hysteria. Some citizens, especially fearful of garrotting, took pre-emptive measures, such as attacking 'suspicious-looking' but entirely innocent passers-by. Inventors rose to the occasion, advertising a range of anti-garrotting devices – belt pistols, anti-garrotte collars and handheld weapons. It was a profitable time for the bodyguarding business too – burly men would escort 'elderly or nervous persons' in the streets after dark. The government gave way to the mood of the day with the Garrotter's Act of 1863, which sanctioned the flogging of garrotters. The monthly figures on 'garrotting' peaked at 32 in November 1862, falling away to just two in January 1863. The panic was over – quite a storm in a teacup.

An important strand of any moral panic is rumour and gossip, but as Stanley Cohen observed, it is the mass media that are key in framing and propagating panics. In journalistic lore exaggerating a scare makes far better copy than good news. Indeed, many popular media outlets thrive on moral panics because they combine entertainment and alarm, fear and fascination, which sell news. The story can be kept alive by repetition, excluding other news and adding corroborating voices – the 'ordinary' person in the street, the sympathetic politician. Selective quotes from scientific experts lend plausibility to claims while evidence to the contrary, or controversy, is left unmentioned. Social media spread the alarm, which in turn delivers more material for the news journalist – a mutually reinforcing relationship.

The trademark of panic reporting is a spiky, inflammatory account that mixes blame with disapproval. In the nineteenth century syphilis was portrayed as 'the filthy pox'. In the 1980s HIV/AIDS was 'a punishment for sin' and 'a plague', and HIV/AIDS sufferers were 'promiscuous' and 'deviants'.[3] In the twenty-first century there was a return to rebellious youth – 'Rain Rescues Capitalism from Spike-haired Hoard' declared *The Times* in 2001, and 'Hoodie Not a Goodie' condemned *The Sun* in 2007. The alarmist rhetoric follows a well-trodden path: it inflates the size of the phenomenon and the danger posed, and uses eye-catching hyperbole. Terms such as 'epidemic proportions' and 'catastrophic' may bear little resemblance to the statistical magnitude of the phenomenon. Critical, reflective journalism generally avoids hitting the panic button, but that does mean it is read neutrally. Readers, as audience theory tells us, are not passive recipients of a storyline: they will take from it the meaning that fits their own preconceptions, even if the actual thrust of the article happens to be in the opposite direction.[4]

Moral panic news stories have, in journalists' jargon, issue-attention cycles. For example, in the 1980s there was moral panic about 'satanic abuse' in the u.s. 'Shocking recovered memories' were elicited from children and adults about demonic rituals, cannibalism and flying witches. Tabloid newspapers were emblazoned with sensationalist headlines and, in an ethos of rising Christian evangelicalism in the u.s., alarm bells rang, which soon spread abroad. But by the late 1980s it was clear that there was no corroborating evidence to support the allegations and the recovered memory methodology was roundly discredited. There was no satanic abuse. The media coverage subsided and by the early 1990s the panic was over.

Some panics vanish almost as rapidly as they appear, soon to be forgotten. Others resonate far longer because they attract the attention of moral watchdogs, people who add authority to the media clamour – heads of churches, chiefs of police, government ministers. They will ride the media swell and push for 'decisive action to tackle the problem', with public opinion in mind. Engineering moral panics can be good news for the news industry, even if the panics are eventually proven unwarranted. Apart from helping the bottom line, they can increase news proprietors' and editors' influence over national agendas and thus generate more news material.

New Folk Devils, New Panics

In August 2001, 438 Afghanistan refugees, including 46 children and three pregnant women, were rescued from their sinking boat by a Norwegian freighter. They were seeking asylum in Australia and were in wretched condition. Some were unconscious; many had skin diseases, hypothermia and diarrhoea. Yet Australia's prime minister, John Howard, ordered his crack sas troops into action to intercept the ship and prevent it from landing the 'boat people' on Australian territory. He accused the refugees of trying to violate Australia's border and 'queue jumping' ahead of more patient refugees. He said that he needed to protect the nation's sovereignty, and anyway the detention centres were full and there could be terrorists among the boat people.[5] In a nutshell, a pitiful group of refugees was equated with an invasion force to be militarily repelled. The response resonated with historical attempts to keep Australia predominantly white and anxieties about foreigners diluting national identity.

Asylum seekers excite xenophobia, especially when they are the 'wrong kind' by dint of country of provenance, ethnicity, colour or religion. As the number of forcibly displaced people on the planet has grown, fears are stirred in wealthy Western nations that the trickle of refugees on their doorstep will turn into a flood and that the social fabric of the nation will suffer, even collapse. Helping others in distress may be a good thing, but not if they are a significant threat to one's way of life. The ingredients of moral panic are in place:

'Asylum tearing UK apart!', *The Sun* (8 May 2003)

'Soft-touch Britain, the asylum seeker capital of Europe: We let in more than anyone else last year', *Daily Mail* (6 June 2012)

'[W]hen assessed as a whole, the evidence of discriminatory, sensational or unbalanced reporting in relation to ethnic minorities, immigrants and/or asylum seekers, is concerning', Lord Justice Leveson, *An Inquiry into the Culture, Practices and Ethics of the Press* (November 2012)

Single incidents of abuse of the asylum system are magnified to caricature all asylum seekers: they are not to be trusted and are into crime and other deviant behaviours. An analysis of Scottish newspapers in 2000 revealed that negative coverage of asylum seekers significantly outweighed positive or balanced stories. Asylum seekers were regularly accused of 'milking the system' and being 'scroungers'.[6] Rarely mentioned was the context of ethnic conflict or civil war, what asylum seekers were actually experiencing or suffering, or that most asylum seekers wanted to return to their homes when peace and stability resumed.

Seeking protection from persecution because of one's race, religion, sexuality, social group or political opinion is one of the most desperate of human acts, a centuries-old phenomenon that is heightened in times of civil unrest and war. Asylum seekers will often stake all on a passage to somewhere they hope will be safe and welcoming. Granting asylum is fundamentally a humanitarian act, understood by signatories to the United Nations Convention on Refugees, but its realpolitik tells a different story. There are nations that will willingly open their doors, but in others populist fears are stirred to present asylum seekers as potential threats and, in moral panic, to shut them out.

Blame the Muslims

The history of nationhood is stained with recrimination between religions, and between religions and states. All that we have observed so far about folk devils applies to this picture: the othering and demonization of a people or group who do not share one's religious or civic values. In recent years Islamophobia has taken central stage, defining much of racial politics in the West. Journalism's 'truths' and Western cultural dominance have fuelled perceptions of how Muslims are, especially as a threat to security and to a Western way of life. Since the 2001 attack on the World Trade Center in New York and the London bombings in 2005, fear has shaped the Western reporting of Muslims. A detailed analysis of tabloid and broadsheet newspapers in the UK over a single week in 2006 revealed 352 stories about Islam and Muslims, 91 per cent of which were negative.[7] Muslims were commonly associated with words such as terrorist, extremist, Islamist, suicide bomber and militant, with very few positive descriptions. Headlines shouted warnings about the Muslim 'takeover': 'Practising Muslims "Will Outnumber Christians" by 2035' (*Daily Telegraph*, 8 May); 'Muslim Britain is Becoming One Big No-go Area' (*Sunday Times*, 13 January); 'Archbishop of Canterbury Warns Sharia Law Is Inevitable' (*The Independent*, 8 February). In her book *Londonistan*, Melanie Phillips laments the decline of Christianity and British national values now usurped, she claims, by Islamic 'colonies' and a 'terror state' in major parts of London.[8]

There is a widespread perception that there can be no common ground between Muslims and non-Muslims, a conviction held by those who admit to knowing little about Islam beyond what they read in the papers; and what they read is not usually flatter-ing.[9] In the u.s. fringe, anti-Islam groups have been effective in getting their agenda over-represented in the media, creating the impression that Muslims are major threats out to destroy every-thing that is fine and good in American society.[10] And in Australia, where Muslims make up less than 2 per cent of the population, they see themselves labelled and vilified by the media, exploit-ing community fears. Their achievements and the positive aspects of their religion are rarely mentioned; ordinary Muslims are marginalized.[11]

In an Islamophobic frenzy, specific cultural practices are singled out, such as the wearing of the burqa – which is por-trayed as oppressive and menacing, rarely as a sign of prized virtue. Mosques and Islamic schools have suffered a similar fate, assumed to be crucibles for radical, hard-line Islamism. For example in January 2012 the headline story from the Swiss news network The Local was 'Radical Muslims Plan Biggest Swiss Mosque', accompanied by a library image of a Muslim priest gesticulating from a pulpit. Switzerland had already banned minaret con-struction, a move condemned by the un Human Rights Council as Islamophobic, and widely regarded as contrary to Switzerland's constitution that guarantees freedom of religion.

Another example is from Australia. In October 2007 a charity submitted a proposal to build an Islamic school within the predominantly Christian community of Camden, a quiet suburb on the fringes of Sydney. It was to be for kindergarten children through to high school, and not a place of worship. Fear and panic aptly describes what followed. The Australian *Telegraph* proclaimed 'Simmering Racial Tensions Set to Explode in Camden' (14 January 2008), and that 'Churches Unite Against Islam School in Camden' (22 April 2009). Protest social media sites sprang up, and there was widespread radio and television coverage. Some 3,000 letters were written to the town council, many objecting to the proposal in undisguised Islamophobic terms: 'Do the Muslims come to Australia to be Australians? No. They come to Australia as forward troops of an eventual occupation'; 'No Muslim school or anything else related to Muslims. Send them home.' To drive their point home protestors impaled two pigs' heads on poles with an Australian flag draped between them and installed them on the site of the proposed school. Meanwhile, nationalistic politicians entered the fray, lending their voices to the protest. Camden Council rejected the proposal 'on planning grounds'.

Islamophobia is an especially stiff broom that sweeps all before it. It is a gut reaction to horrific world events that are reported selectively and then lumped together to suggest a picture of what all Muslims are like. Fear and loathing can soon swamp the niceties of who is and is not blameworthy within a Muslim community; it is easier to generalize. The Muslim majority, moderate in their beliefs and peaceful in their ways, can struggle to be heard. Indeed, when Muslims in the u.s. have been asked their views on radical violence, a higher proportion than of any other religious group deplore the targeting or killing of civilians by individuals or small groups; they also disown any sympathy for al-Qaeda.[12] And here lies the crux of Islamophobia: the spread of blame from those rightly castigated for carrying out or sponsoring atrocities in the name of Islam – the suicide bombers, the radical priests, the jihadist training camps, the states that back violence – to blaming everyone of the Islamic faith for their 'radicalism'. The media's role cannot be over-stated; stories that provoke community anxiety are part and parcel of news-making politics. Some are tendentious to the point of absurdity. Scanty intelligence about Muslim terrorists has been fed by governments to information-starved journalists, who report it as authoritative; it is then used by governments as evidence why they should deport Muslims.[13]

We have to look beyond sensationalism for more thoughtful accounts. Some analyses point to the discriminatory structures of a nation. In France, for example, Islam is the second most widely practised religion; however, Muslims have struggled to find work and be accepted into mainstream culture, turning inwards to their own ethnic culture for identity and support – taken by Islamophobes as proof that Muslims do not want to assimilate. In Britain the picture is not dissimilar. There are young, educated Muslims who have found their social mobility blocked and have felt out of place in British society; in frustration a number have been attracted to radical Islamic voices. We are here reminded of the cultural diversity of Muslims – the Sub-Saharan Muslims in Paris, Somali Muslims in London, Moroccan Muslims in Amsterdam and Turkish Muslims in Berlin. All have experiences that reflect their own backgrounds and local history, differences conveniently overlooked by the Islamophobe.

Blame the Paedophiles

The panic over paedophilia in recent years has raised the alarm about a practice that has been shrouded in secrecy and historically under-reported. It has drawn attention to the lifelong damage that paedophilia can inflict on its victims and raised searching questions about how society protects its children. Is this, then, an example of moral panic where the benefits outweigh the costs?

The term 'paedophilia' became prominent in the 1990s as news outlets, government officials and various professional organizations raised concerns. In the UK, headlines reached panic proportions in the late 1990s. The *News of the World* was a major player when, in July 2000, it informed its readers that 'thousands' of paedophiles were preying on young children. It published the names, photographs and whereabouts of some of the likely offenders, despite official warnings that this could increase the danger to children by driving offenders underground. The *Daily Mirror* added its front-page opinion that 'Hanging These Bastards Really is Too Good for Them'.[14] One effect was to galvanize lynch mobs that set fire to the homes of supposed sex offenders. The home of a hospital paediatrician was also attacked, her professional title confused with 'paedophile'.

In the subsequent decade, paedophilia panic surfaced worldwide after disclosures of historical child sexual abuse by priests and children sexually abused in care homes. Vigilante groups began entrapping paedophiles, including the entirely innocent.[15] In the UK the furore was stoked with startling revelations about a much-feted British television celebrity, Jimmy Savile. Following his death in 2011 it transpired that he had lived a parallel life as a serial sexual predator of children, many encounters dating back to the 1960s and '70s. Over a long period he had sexually abused scores of vulnerable youngsters under the cover of his high-profile persona: a popular-music celebrity who advocated for children's charities and hospitals. His victims would only speak out after his death, having previously felt intimidated by him and been convinced – with justification – that they would not be believed. A chill wind blew across associates of Jimmy Savile, as well as others in the popular music and media industry. For some, the so-called liberal sexual norms of the 1960s had returned to haunt them; they were now potential child abusers and the police were on their trail.

Another fall-out of the paedophile panic was to render suspect hitherto innocuous behaviour, such as strangers comforting a distressed child in the street or watching children at play in a school playground or park. One elderly man related the following tale to me:

> I was doing what I've done for years – a mid-morning stroll down to the esplanade of Brighton beach, very near where I live. It's always buzzing with different sorts of people doing things. I love it there. I sat down on my usual bench which happens to overlook a small green where children play, some with their parents, some with their friends – there's lots of play equipment there. It's great to see them so happy. I stayed there for my usual 40 minutes or so and then began to walk slowly home. Suddenly a police car pulled up beside me and a policewoman got out and demanded my identification. I was flabbergasted. 'Why?' I asked. Because, she said, someone had called them complaining that I was staring at children for a long time. She was eventually convinced I was no threat to mankind, let alone children, but I was really distressed and depressed at what had happened. What on earth is things coming to if you can't sit on a bench and look at some kids playing![16]

Paedophilia taps a deep vein of revulsion, but when it is presented in melodramatic form accusations fly in all directions. Like grapeshot from an old-fashioned cannon, some hit the desired target, but pity the innocent passer-by. Nevertheless, could the paedophilia alarm be an instance of a defensible moral panic? It has raised the political, legal and psychological profile of child abuse. It has rooted out destructive and nefarious conduct among some of the most socially prestigious groups in society. It has thrown light on the murky world of online child-stalkers and Internet rings. It has been a sharp shot in the arm for protective agencies – police, social work, child care. Child protection services are now more focused on identifying vulnerable children and their abusers and many schools have become proactive in advising children how to keep safe, especially from grooming websites. It is likely that none of this would have happened without intense media attention and the stirring of public anger and disgust. The moral panic is vindicated.

Yet questions remain. While protecting potential victims is essential, a spotlight on the individual paedophile and their 'twisted' character limits our understanding of the phenomenon, and ultimately its prevention. Not all paedophiles are manipulative and aggressive; many, contrary to stereotype, are gentle and caring and not exclusively attracted to children.[17] Professional opinion is divided about the causes of paedophilia. Some see it as a mental illness or deviancy, others as a product of cycles of abuse, and still others as an abnormality in development.[18] However, a common thread is that the paedophile cannot be blamed for a sexual desire they did not choose or cannot help feeling; but they can be held responsible for acting on their urges, and offered help on how to deal with them.[19]

Scaremongering about paedophilia creates a disproportionate response by which innocent, commonplace behaviours become suspect: the blameless become scapegoats for a few over-reported cases. Meanwhile, in concentrating on individual culprits, attention is deflected from the culpability of organizations that turn a blind eye to the paedophilic behaviour in their midst.

3

Blame Cultures

'Whose fault is it?' This is a familiar refrain when something goes wrong in an organization. Find the perpetrator and admonish them. If the offence is serious there should be tougher sanctions – perhaps demotion or dismissal. This done, the organization can continue its business as usual.

Individualizing blame in this way is consistent with the way we use blame in our lives generally. The same dynamics are at play, save one key difference – the influence of the organization's culture. A blame-free organization is neither realistic nor desirable; without sanctions for reckless behaviour the credibility of the organization is at stake, not least in the eyes of its members. If someone has wilfully ignored a key operating principle or rule, deliberately evaded core responsibilities or broken the law, blame is rightly due. Yet when blaming is the dominant reflex, the way an organization characteristically approaches its staff, we can speak meaningfully of a blame culture.

Blame cultures typically filter from the top of an organization, from a leader who rebukes people for their mistakes rather than recognizing them for their achievements, a 'who broke . . .' rather than 'how to fix . . .' approach. Blame cultures are sclerotic; they foster fear and scapegoating; people are reluctant to admit mistakes and are prone to pass the buck. It makes little sense to report work difficulties if they are going to be thrown back in your face; it makes little sense to try out new ideas if you are blamed if they do not work out. In short, blame cultures shut down personal initiative and encourage self-protection. They create what psychology professor James Reason calls 'a vulnerable systems syndrome': the organization becomes more prone to dysfunction and blunders.[1] This can be catastrophic in times of crisis when an out-of-the-ordinary response is imperative – precisely what a blame culture cannot deliver.

Blame's Blind Spots

On 6 March 1987 the roll-on roll-off passenger and freight ferry *Herald of Free Enterprise* left Zeebrugge, bound for Dover. Some four minutes later it capsized and 193 people perished; the bow loading doors had been left open. The assistant bosun was directly responsible for closing them, but he was asleep in his cabin at the time. 'He will,' concluded the court of inquiry, 'no doubt, suffer remorse for a long time to come.' That could have been the end of the matter. However, it was discovered that a more senior crewman had noticed that the doors were open but had done nothing because, he said, it had never been part of his duties. Neither was it anyone's duty to tell the captain whether or not the bow doors were safely closed, something which had been identified at an earlier date by another captain in the fleet. Management, 'infected with the disease of sloppiness', had ignored his request to install warning lights. An inherent design fault in the ship was also established, predisposing it to capsize if flooded.

We can rightly blame the assistant bosun for his disastrous failure of duty: he triggered the tragedy. But he was clearly only part of the story. Indeed, over 30 years of research on major accidents and disasters shows that pinning the blame on the most obvious culprit is no guarantee that the calamity will not recur. Yet we still often fail to look beyond a fall guy. An individual to blame gives an impression of closure, relieves others of culpability and quietens press speculation. However, it obscures the fact that the potential for calamity often lies hidden, or ignored, in the interstices of an organization.

Just Cultures

The opposite of a blame culture is one where people feel free to admit errors and make suggestions; they can join with others in tackling problems. It is not blame free but is fundamentally open, inclusive and fair; in a word, it is 'just'. A 'just culture' encourages organizational members to voice their criticisms, complaints, warnings or mistakes without fear of reproach or victimization. Individuals are not blamed for breakdowns or blunders over which they have no control, and there is a deeper and historical analysis of what has gone wrong.[2] Just cultures make the most of 'double-loop learning', where an analyst (manager, investigator, employee) returns to the scene of the crime, so to speak, and explores the wider context, background policies and assumptions that made the event possible in the first place.[3] It contrasts with the much narrower single-loop learning, which identifies and blames a perpetrator and looks no further.

Moving from a blame culture to a just culture challenges ingrained habits and vested interests. Top-level commitment is vital, building awareness throughout the organization, supported by education and training. Symbols of the old culture, such as punishment protocols, written reprimands and dismissal after a certain number of infractions, need to be removed. As with all cultural changes, it is actual deeds, not just declarations, that make it convincing and trustworthy to participants.

In practice, the pace and form of just cultures vary according to the particular industry or service. Often there has been a piecemeal or 'first step' response rather than a complete shift in culture. In civil aviation, for instance, pilots, air traffic controllers and other frontline staff have been reluctant to report problems that might be self-incriminatory because they can be automatically prosecuted following an air incident. The International Civil Aviation Organization has urged countries to create a legal framework for just cultures where 'staff are not punished for actions, omissions or decisions taken by them that are commensurate with their experience and training, but where gross negligence, wilful violations and destructive acts are not tolerated'.[4] Some military air forces have already moved in this direction, such as the Canadian Air Force. Its flight safety programme maintains the anonymity of staff who report errors and omissions and does not assign blame, and reports cannot be used for disciplinary or legal proceedings.

Other organizations have experimented with 'safety huddles' – bringing together staff from across the organization in a blameless environment. Carefully led, they can break down the silos that divide workers and help them share their knowledge about errors or near misses that affect safety or the like. Bureaucracy is minimized and informal notes are favoured over formal minutes. They can be found in some medical settings. For example, physicians working in a Boston perinatal unit were failing to notice patient contra-indications because of high workloads and fatigue. Nursing staff were aware of the problem but were reluctant to challenge or blame their superiors, and the medical culture militated against physicians criticizing one another. The administration's response was to introduce twice-daily 'board rounds', a cell of safety where nurses, alongside physicians and residents in training, could speak their minds without fear of criticism. Patient care plans and physicians' schedules were reviewed and amended where necessary.[5]

Another example is social work. Social workers typically operate under difficult, pressurized conditions and are held individually responsible for the outcomes of their complex casework. A UK social work department was facing cases that had gone seriously wrong, but instead of lining up practitioners to be judged in the usual manner, they were brought together with a team of senior managers to openly share their experiences without recrimination. They explored what affected the decisions and the worries they had at the time. Reactions to the approach were predominantly of relief. In the words of one social worker, 'You don't feel you are being blamed. You are really able to dissect the decisions you have made, which helps you to reflect not just on that case, but also on current cases.'[6]

Profiting from Blame

There is money to be made from blame, a fact long known to aggrieved divorcees and disgruntled employees in North America. Financial damages have become a defining characteristic of a blame-and-compensation culture, now on both sides of the Atlantic.

An organization's vulnerability to blame increases as health and safety requirements become more stringent while, at the same time, employees and consumers become more aware of their legal rights. Unusual or quirky cases often make the news – like the British teacher who slipped on a chip (french fry) in 2005 and strained her knee ligaments. It happened on a ramp outside her school canteen where the colour and pattern of the tiled flooring camouflaged the chip. She was awarded £55,000.[7] In 2007 another British teacher, desperate for the toilet, rushed to the nearest one – designed for her junior pupils' small bodies. She fell off her perch and dislocated her hip and was awarded £14,000 in damages.[8] These are sizeable compensations, but pale into insignificance compared to some u.s. settlements, such as the nearly $3 million awarded to a 79-year-old woman in the 1990s after she spilled a very hot cup of McDonald's coffee over her groin area.[9]

Not all cases go the litigant's way. McDonald's was again in the spotlight in 2003 when New Yorker Israel Bradley went to court to accuse McDonald's of responsibility for his teen-age daughter's obesity. Nineteen-stone (270 lb/120 kg) Jazlyn lived on a diet of McMuffins and Big Macs: 'I always believed McDonald's was healthy for my children', claimed Bradley.[10] The judge ruled that, on this occasion, it was the individual's responsibility to know where to draw the line. Another lost cause was Lauren Rosenberg's quarrel with Google. She used her

BlackBerry to download Google Maps for walking directions to her destination in Utah. Along the way it instructed her to walk down a rural highway that had no sidewalk or pedestrian paths. She did what it said and was struck by a car. She sued the driver for damages, and also Google for its unsafe directions. In a lengthy summing up the judge rejected her case against Google.[11]

A bullish compensation industry normalizes events such as these. Compensation 'consultants' proliferate, such as the National Accident Helpline – 'Did you know: two and a half million people in the UK are injured in accidents every year? And only 6 per cent are fully aware of their legal rights regarding personal injury claims.' And Claims Direct ('no win no fee'), whose website lists 37 different categories of claim that it is happy to deal with, from whiplash, burns and cycling accidents to stress at work, slipping, poisoning and faulty products. For the unsure there is a 'simply click on the area of the body' image that says how much their injury is worth.

Employers and major institutions are often seen as fair game in these adversarial adventures: 'They and their insurers can afford it.' BP felt cast in this light following its Gulf of Mexico disaster in 2010, an oil spill that, in addition to environmental harm, damaged the livelihood of commercial fisherman, restaurateurs and hotel owners. But precisely which ones? And what were their actual losses? As the list of compensation claimants grew to 170,000, BP and its lawyers became aware of 'dozens of inflated and even fictitious claims'. Given the enormity of the oil spill, few were sympathetic to BP's complaints. However, the spectre of people profiting from illegitimate claims, possibly at the expense of those suffering genuine losses, reveals the allure of 'something for nothing' that attends the compensation culture. It was a driver behind the UK's unflattering reputation as 'the whiplash capital of Europe' in the 2000s. Between 2005 and 2011 the number of road accidents in the UK fell markedly, but claims for whiplash injuries to the head and neck increased, at one point running at 1,500 a day. Doctors, some with a regular client base of solicitors, could command a fee for processing the claims, and because whiplash is hard to disprove most claims were waved through. The point was not lost on criminal gangs who staged vehicle shunts on the highway and then claimed whiplash damages for themselves. One audacious attempt involved packing a local bus that normally carried no more than six to eight people with 30 pre-briefed 'passengers'. A minor collision was arranged, resulting in 30 identical claims for injuries.[12]

Hypercaution

Compensation for genuinely defective or damaging products or services is a feature of a robust, ethical economy, increasing the accountability of providers. But a compensation culture distorts this. It fosters a parasitical economy that feeds off and distorts the true economy. Many ordinary risks of life become opportunities to exploit – legally or illegally – to make a quick buck.

Unsurprisingly, there has been a backlash in the shape of the super-cautious organization. Hazards, however slight, are removed, spawning apocryphal tales about who is or is not allowed to use a stepladder, boil a kettle or change a light bulb. The traditional school trip, adventure playground or children's sport has fallen foul of the trend, judged by some educational authorities as too risky to continue. Civic administrators have viewed autumn warily, with public notices such as 'Beware Falling Conkers – Please Proceed with Care', and 'Caution – Please Be Aware of the Falling Acorns'.[13] The natural delights of conkers and acorns are redefined as security and compensation risks.

For some time, client-facing workers have had to adjust to the prospect of lawsuits and compensation claims. Lawyers, accountants, psychiatrists, psychologists and estate agents (realtors) are especially vulnerable, and physicians top the list. The traditional image of the doctor as an aloof, god-like figure has given way to a more sceptical perception: they make mistakes; they are blameable; they are suable. 'It is very difficult', confessed a British general practitioner with twenty years' experience, 'to keep up that energy and that politeness and that open friendliness if you feel that as soon as there is any little glitch then actually they're going to blame you.'[14] Alleged malpractice casts the deepest shadow, as one doctor relates:

> Being sued comes with a terrible stigma. As soon as you open the envelope, you can feel your heart drop a thousand fathoms as the black oil slick of doubt seeps into fissures of your mind. Your thoughts steep in terror, your mind leaping to possibility; I'm done for, what's going to happen, this is the end of my career, how will I survive . . . what if I lose? You don't want to know that truth. You don't want to walk there. And so you go through the motions with visceral pain until it's all over, and then bow your head, your self-worth and will power ripped from your heart.[15]

Defensive medicine reduces some of these risks. It has the appearance of thoroughness, with lots of diagnostic tests, procedures and specialist consultations – but they are medically unnecessary. They are there primarily to protect the practitioner. It has become customary to ask a patient to sign a legal waiver form before their surgical operation, while some physicians choose to avoid high-risk patients when the outcomes of medical procedures are uncertain.

Defensive medicine is largely global, present in the UK, U.S., Australia, New Zealand, Israel, Japan and Germany. A recent survey found 78 per cent of medical doctors in the UK practising it in one form or another.[16] Likewise, in the U.S., many neurosurgeons and physicians report that they resort to defensive medicine, ordering more tests than are medically required.[17] Nurses and hospital administrators there see fear of litigation as the major reason.[18] Defensive medicine inflates the costs of the American healthcare system, one estimate putting the annual bill at $55.6 billion.[19]

Audits – More Blame?

Auditors can pinpoint an organization's strengths and weakness and where any blame or responsibility should be directed for, say, malpractice, illegal acts or conflicts of interest. Independent, external auditing has long been a mainstay of corporate account-ability and is vital to public trust, a process complemented by internal auditors, responsible to the board of directors. As con-cern has grown about ineffective, unethical or corrupt practices in private and public organizations, the role of auditors has expanded as a prime means of boosting accountability and good governance.

But, according to Professor Michael Power of the London School of Economics, it does not always work out that way. Our 'audit society' aims to increase transparency but often results in the opposite because it stokes blame cultures and defensive practices. Power describes the 'typical' auditee:

> The auditee is undoubtedly a complex being: simultaneously devious and depressed; she is skilled at games of compliance but exhausted and cynical about them too; she is nervous about the empty certificates of comfort that get produced but she also colludes in amplifying audit mandates in local settings . . . she knows public accountability and stakeholder dialogue are good things but wonders why, after all her years of training, she is not trusted as an expert anymore.[20]

Those on the receiving end of regular inspections and audits describe them as at best ritualistic and at worst dispiriting. Public healthcare worldwide has borne the major brunt of inquiries and audits, each review generating a new regime of audit tools and checklists, described in a Swedish study as a 'documentation hysteria' that consumes at least 25 per cent of normal working time.[21] Auditees worry about being blamed and scapegoated for unavoidable mistakes or for the shortcomings of their organization. 'Massaged' reports and compliance games to give the impression that imposed targets have been met have become commonplace. In interactions with auditors, some auditees will try to influence matters in their own favour, such as being selective with the facts or by exploiting weaknesses in the auditor's control system.[22]

These perverse consequences are illustrated by what happened within the police services of England and Wales in the early 2000s. They were audited on their crime detection rates, a key public indicator of their performance. In response, the police became wary about what they did or did not report, and there were instances of switching to 'soft' offences that could boost their detection rates. Professor Irvine Lapsley of Edinburgh University cites the arrest of a child who removed a slice of cucumber from a tuna mayonnaise sandwich and threw it at another youngster. And there was the man cautioned by police for being 'in possession of an egg with intent to throw'.[23] Even more 'rewarding' was a situation in which a single detection could be expanded into a multiple one:

> The operation began after a child was accused of keeping £700 raised for Comic Relief through sponsorship. Police officers were sent to talk to every person who had sponsored the child to bump up their targets. They spent two weeks on door-to-door enquiries sending community police officers to get 542 crimes. Five hundred is better than one.[24]

Audits walk a thin line between providing all stakeholders with important, valid information and creating regimes that undermine the very trust necessary to make them worthwhile.

4

Blaming the Organization

Organizations get blamed for many things – unethical or illegal practices, exploitation of workers, destruction of the environment, unreliable products, false or broken promises. Large corporations and private utilities are especially vulnerable, the 'most hated' appearing from time to time in the press.[1] Strongest criticism is usually reserved for companies linked to child labour, pornography, animal harm, arms, abortion or tobacco. Being socially responsible has become part of the rhetoric of modern management, yet there is no automatic obligation on a company to behave virtuously. In corporate law a company has a major duty to maximize its value to its shareholders, where 'value' for many shareholders is getting the best and quickest financial return on their investment. Moreover, the Milton Friedman school of economics – 'the social responsibility of business is to increase its profits' – still reverberates in some business quarters, where the costs of pollution, community dislocation and worker protection are externalized wherever possible, leaving society to pick up the pieces.

The Blamers

Corporatization insinuates itself into our lives. It is a charge that unites corporate critics, such as George Monbiot (*Captive State*), Noreen Hertz (*The Silent Takeover*), Eveline Lubbers (*Battling Big Business*) and Naomi Klein (*No Logo*). Klein has been particularly vocal. She sets her sights on the supermarket chains, superstores, fast-food franchises and coffee outlets that 'brand bomb' us with their ubiquitous presence, sited in multiple locations at home and abroad. They saturate our brand awareness, numbing us into brand acceptance and complacency. What we fail to notice, or would prefer not to know, suggests Klein, is the vast amount that they spend on branding and how the corporate brand and profits are often sustained by a low-cost, casualized labour force with poor – or no – security. A rigidly controlled supply chain extends to developing countries where local workers are readily exploited by outsourced local agents.

Critics point to the spillover from corporate branding, from the rights to name a sports stadium to the provision of educational material such as schoolbooks, teaching packs and tokens for special equipment – irresistible to some financially strapped schools. McDonald's, for example, describes itself, with some accuracy, as one of the best-known brands in the world. It offers material to 'enhance classroom studies', which includes information on nutrition and the environment, long-time touchy areas for the company. It is an exercise in soft marketing – enticing children to their brand but with a socially responsible gloss.[2]

In concentrating power, many corporations appear untouchable. A multinational's revenues can outstrip those of a nation state: General Electric's value is greater than the gross domestic product of New Zealand; Ford is worth more than Morocco; Apple more than Poland; Amazon more than Kenya; McDonald's more than Latvia; and Exxon Mobil more than Thailand. Much of this wealth and muscle is protected by corporate law. In the U.S. corporations are treated as 'juristic persons', a curious construction that gives them constitutional rights of their own and makes them accountable only to their shareholders.[3]

When a major corporation is openly challenged it can muster considerable resources in its defence. If taken to court by aggrieved individuals or communities it can assemble a potent legal team to fight its corner, often watering down any settlements. One example has been Union Carbide's response to the Bhopal tragedy. Toxic gases from Union Carbide's pesticide plant drifted over the slumbering city of Bhopal in 1984. The official tally of deaths was 2,259, although other sources put the number as high as 8,000.[4] Over time the poison debilitated an estimated further 16,000 people.[5] The company offered a legal settlement of $350 million, which was rejected by the Indian government acting on behalf of claimants; it proposed compensation of $3.3 billion. An out of court settlement of $470 million was reached five years after the disaster, a fraction of the government's original claim.[6] Further appeals from victims failed, as did initial attempts to hold key executives to account.[7] It was 26 years before senior officials of Union Carbide's Indian subsidiary were successfully prosecuted, but not the company's American former chief. He was arrested on a visit to India, skipped bail and returned to the U.S., which refused to extradite him.[8]

Exxon's notorious oil spill followed a not dissimilar path. In 1989 the *Exxon Valdez* oil tanker struck a reef in Prince William Sound, Alaska, polluting 1,330 miles (2,140 km) of pristine coastline and 11,000 square miles (28,500 square km) of ocean. The direct damage and attendant losses to fishermen and other small businesses were so severe that, in 1994, a court decreed the largest punitive award in U.S. history – $5 billion.[9] There followed years of appeals by Exxon, and in 2008 the U.S. Supreme Court massively reduced its liability to $507.5 million.[10] On the 25th anniversary of the disaster, $92 million dollars of this is still disputed – amid authoritative reports of still-fresh oil in Prince William Sound.[11]

The Whistle-blower

On the night of 27 November 2003, Satyendra Kumar Dubey waited for his usual car to pick him up from the railway station and take him home after work. It failed to arrive; the driver 'couldn't start it up'. He took a rickshaw instead, but he never made it home. Armed men intercepted him and shot him dead.

Dubey was a young manager employed by the National Highways Authority of India, overseeing a major highways project, a pet project of the Prime Minister. Dubey had become so concerned about the poor quality of the workmanship that he insisted that major sections were redone. He was also very worried about corruption and bribery surrounding the project, especially the sub-contracting of work to inferior operators – a not uncommon practice in India.

He voiced his concerns to his immediate superiors, but there was no response. He then wrote directly to the Prime Minister's Office and to Chairman of the National Highways Authority, mentioning also that he had been receiving threatening calls. In his submission he explained that, 'since such letters from a common man are not usually treated with due seriousness, I wish to clarify . . . that this letter is being written after careful thought by a very concerned citizen who is also very closely linked with the project . . . kindly go through my brief particulars (attached on a separate sheet to ensure secrecy) before proceeding further.'

He asked that his name be kept secret. It was not. The letter and his identity were sent on to others in the labyrinthine bureaucracy of Indian administration, including his superiors. He paid for his whistle-blowing with his life.[12]

• • •

Jeffrey Wigand was President of Research and Development at Brown and Williamson Tobacco Corporation from 1989 to 1993. He had become increasingly alarmed about a cover-up of evidence linking tobacco to health. Attempts to develop a safer cigarette were constantly blocked and he was frustrated in his efforts to raise his concerns internally. He resigned. The company was nervous about his insider knowledge, so they forced him to sign a confidentiality agreement, essentially a gagging order. But he decided that the matter was too important to suppress, so he went public on primetime television. His revelations earned him much public acclaim, but not without considerable personal costs – anonymous death threats aimed at his young daughters (a bullet in his mailbox) and the need for 24-hour bodyguard protection.[13]

What is striking about these accounts, and others like them, is that whistle-blowers put their reputations, careers, families and sometimes lives on the line. Yet they rarely think about it in these terms at the outset. Many know that they are taking a risk but they seldom realize its magnitude. They are doing what any person of scruples should do – report morally dubious or unethical practices; the truth should out. They do not share their colleagues' fatalism – 'oh, nothing can be done' – or fear of speaking out.[14] Some whistle-blowers are rank-and-file workers, but most are senior staff or specialists, such as union representatives, health and safety officers or financial controllers.[15] Invariably it is a lack of internal response that impels them to go outside the organization, or because they feel trapped: required to report a wrongdoing to the very people who are most responsible for it. Contrary to popular belief, whistle-blowers are rarely compulsive attention-seekers, nor are they ingrained malcontents – a description often used to discredit them.[16]

Whistle-blowing takes moral courage. It also takes the wit – or foolhardiness – necessary to swim against the tide of conformity and silence. The barriers can be considerable. Workplace norms generally proscribe telling on a colleague, while the bystander effect – 'someone else, surely, will take action, it doesn't need to be me' – keeps many transgressions and transgressors hidden. There are wider cultural factors too. In parts of Latin America and Asia the scarcity of jobs is such that whistle-blowing may rob someone permanently of their livelihood, while in South Korea, China and Japan it can threaten a collective ethos and bring disgrace to one's community and family.

In Germany, Russia and South Africa it can re-awaken an uncomfortable past of secret informants.

From the organization's perspective, the whistle-blower who 'goes public' has committed the ultimate betrayal. Whatever the rights or wrongs of the matter, you do not wash your organization's dirty linen in public. Retaliation can be swift, including questioning the whistle-blower's mental health (prescribing psychiatric help), marginalizing and diminishing their job, shunning by colleagues, entrapping them with impossible assignments, reassigning them to remote locations and repeated disciplinary action.[17] Government whistle-blowers can be treated especially harshly, as an unassuming army intelligence analyst was to learn. Private Bradley Manning released thousands of confidential u.s. State Department diplomatic cables in 2010, revealing the duplicities of worldwide diplomatic chatter. His action earned him public praise as a beacon of liberty, but condemnation in equal measure by the u.s. State Department. He was convicted of violations of the Espionage Act and sentenced to 35 years in prison.

Whistle-blowing is, therefore, a risky business, but there are whistle-blowers who manage to navigate the obstacles and bring about major changes. They are most celebrated when their cause strikes a popular note and the wrongdoing they expose shocks a nation. It happened thus to Sherron Watkins, Cynthia Cooper and Coleen Rowley. In 2002 all three were hailed by *Time* magazine as 'persons of the year' who 'took huge professional and personal risks', as 'fail-safe systems that did not fail'.[18] Sherron Watkins was vice president of Corporate Development at the mighty Enron Corporation. She alerted her CEO to systematic fraud in the accounting methods of the firm, leading eventually to the firm's collapse.[19] Internal auditor Cynthia Cooper blew the whistle on phoney bookkeeping in the American telecommunications giant WorldCom. She and her team uncovered approximately $3.8 billion of fraud.[20] As a WorldCom employee she did not intend to go public, but a member of Congress released her audit memos to the press. The company collapsed in 2002 and its CEO was convicted of orchestrating the fraud and sentenced to 25 years in prison.[21] Coleen Rowley was a special agent with the FBI who, following the 11 September 2001 attacks, informed the director of the FBI that staff at headquarters had ignored pleas from its own agents to investigate Zacarias Moussaoui, later indicted as a 9/11 co-conspirator. Rowley testified at a Senate hearing on the FBI's mishandling of the affair.[22]

Safer Whistle-blowing?

Some organizations are willing to listen to and learn from internal criticism, encouraging rather than demonizing whistle-blowers: all part of a productive troubleshooting culture. Special grievance committees are created as well as hotlines that bypass the usual management structures. For example, during 2012–13, News Corporation, under the stewardship of Rupert Murdoch, was engulfed in scandals about phone hacking and illegal payments for confidential information. The company's – belated – response was to set up an 'alertline' on which employees could report, 'without retaliation', violations of the company's ethics code.

The credibility of these initiatives hinges upon responding constructively to grievances and revelations. It also means protecting the whistle-blower's identity, occasionally placing the organization in a difficult position. A case arose in the UK when an internal whistle-blower reported two medical consultants for doing private work during National Health Service paid time. The consultants denied the claim but were suspended pending investigations by the NHS's Counter Fraud Squad and forbidden contact with colleagues. The inquiry took three months before concluding that there was no basis for the allegation. The consultants returned to work, but by then their health had suffered and their reputations were damaged. Meanwhile the whistle-blower remained anonymous and untouched. The

Consultants Union were unhappy with the outcome: 'Malicious whistleblowing is destroying consultant careers – and so is the lack of any realistic accountability of the perpetrators.'[23]

There are customer-facing organizations that open channels for customer whistle-blowers. The u.s. Inland Revenue Service, for example, offers payments to individuals who identify fellow citizens who fail to pay their taxes. It disbursed $2.9 billion reward money between 1987 and 2010.[24] The Chinese government, notoriously closed to complaints from its people, has been won over to hotlines where citizens are financially rewarded for reporting proven abuses of power by public officials. Local prosecutors' offices have recorded over 10,000 complaints a year, and more than 6,000 online posts.[25] Enticing whistle-blowers in these ways has the uncomfortable feel of a snooper's charter. On the other hand they could be defended on the grounds that they help serve greater goods from which we all benefit – society's tax revenues and non-corrupt officialdom.

Whistle-blowers are not well protected by law, although some are shielded under clauses on the freedom of speech or employment security. In countries where a dedicated law is in place it does not normally address why a person blew the whistle in the first place but rather the way they were treated afterwards. Tribunals typically require proof from whistle-blowers about when victimization began, in what form and by whom – often contested by well-briefed company lawyers. The problem for whistle-blowers is that most do not think of themselves in these terms at the outset, or consider that it would be prudent to record what is happening in the event that they have to seek redress in court.

Social Pressure Groups

Social pressure groups range from the ad hoc to major international movements. All seek change through targeted confrontation and blame – explicit or implicit. Some are defined by their sectional interests as consumers, workers, patients, the disabled and so forth; they highlight organizations and institutions that fail to meet their basic needs. Some are ideologically driven, opposed to what they regard as the immorality of, say, weapons manufacture, abortion clinics or animal laboratories. Still others focus on how an organization does its business rather than the business per se – through exploitative working conditions, misleading claims, destroying communities, over-fishing or damaging the natural environment. All groups wish to draw attention to their particular cause and call their target to account, but how they do it varies. A number are openly adversarial, others aim to persuade through partnerships, and a third group act as independent watchdogs, to observe and report.

On the Street

The McLibel Two was a major milestone in street protests. In 1990 McDonald's issued writs against two people in the UK, a former postman and a gardener. They had handed out leaflets tantalizingly titled *What's Wrong with McDonald's: Everything They Don't Want You to Know*. The leaflets included allegations about McDonald's addictive junk food, its waste, its exploitation of children and its environmental degradation. The case dragged on for seven long years in a David and Goliath contest where the defendants were denied legal aid, so ran their own defence. A judge finally ruled that some of their accusations were not well founded, so McDonald's had been libelled and the pair should pay damages.[26]

They refused, went to appeal and then to the Court of Human Rights in Strasbourg. There, the original trial was deemed unfair and the defendants were awarded damages and costs. Meanwhile the McLibel Two had become popular heroes. Anti-McDonald's press reports mushroomed and a feature-length documentary was made about the case. The reputational damage to McDonald's was considerable.[27]

A few years later, on the other side of the Atlantic, another fast-food protest was brewing, this time against the giant corporation Taco Bell. Activists accused Taco Bell of grossly abusing their Florida-based tomato pickers, alleging that they were among the most exploited in the u.s.[28] Their cause was taken up by student and community sympathizers and, in 2001, was dramatized by hunger-striking workers outside Taco Bell headquarters in California. The company faced a three-year boycott before it eventually acceded to the workers' demands with a pay rise of some 70 per cent.[29]

A final example returns us to the UK: a citizens' protest against Tesco, one that resonates with Naomi Klein's trenchant critique of the supermarket industry. Tesco accounts for some 30 per cent of the grocery market in the UK with nearly 3,000 outlets. The company's business methods and appetite for expansion have met with resistance from many groups, including trade unions, Friends of the Earth and War on Want. Local activists have been particularly vocal, alarmed by Tesco's effects on independent businesses and the cloning of high streets into brand-similarity. Tescopoly Alliance, a 'resource website' for local campaigners, summarizes the disquiet:

> There are concerns that the closure of small shops is a one-way street. Once small independent stores shut, there are often insurmountable barriers to getting back into the high street. It is very difficult for new businesses to start up. And there are concerns that a tipping point could be reached. Once a certain amount of independent retailers shut, the wholesale industry may no longer be sustainable, and could collapse.[30]

The citizens of Bristol confronted this very prospect in 2011. A local campaign was waged against Tesco's plans to open a new convenience store in a socially mixed, 'alternative' neighbourhood, close to the city centre. The store was modest in size but substantial in symbolism. The locality was already well served by an assortment of independent food shops and supermarkets. In the eyes of many local residents Tesco was an example of the failure of local government to counter corporate power. Resistance began as low-key and good-natured. Campaigners distributed leaflets ('Think local, boycott Tesco') and paraded Tesco-parodying banners ('Stop Tesco, Every Little Hurts', a corruption of Tesco's marketing slogan, 'Every Little Helps'). Soon less peaceful participants appeared on the scene, attracted by the flurry of social media messages. As the days passed the protest became tenser, eventually to transform into a full-scale riot. The store was thoroughly wrecked.[31]

At one level the protest failed. It was unable to prevent the store from eventually operating a year later, and the cause was tarnished by media images of riots. At another level it was a salutary, and very public, message to other communities and Tesco executives about Tesco's diminishing social capital. It also prompted active discussions between the local community and municipal council on a new vision for development of the area.[32]

These cases demonstrate how spontaneous street actions can stall or reverse corporate decisions and inflict reputational damage. In terms of the politics of protest, they hold a number of cards. They challenge carefully polished corporate claims about social responsibility; they have an immediacy and urgency, especially when orchestrated through blogs and text messaging; and they attract the attention of media, sometimes transforming a local protest into a national or international one. Not all media outlets are necessarily sympathetic to a particular cause, but no matter; as the adage goes, bad publicity can be better than no publicity at all. The important thing for protesters is that they are reported because it raises public awareness about their concerns.

Changing Tactics

After the McLibel Two, street campaigners have been wary about making accusations that can be contested in court. Indeed, many major street events are now carnivalesque – peaceful marches, sits-ins, encampments, theatricality and music – all purposefully irreverent towards their target of blame. A participant in one of London's Carnivals Against Capitalism describes the atmosphere:

> The Carnival kicks off in Liverpool Street station and the drums are loud and thrilling on the stone floor. It's as though the huge concourse, designed for the discomfort of travellers, has just been waiting all these years for a rave. Here it is, and we snake out with the drums to a dead plaza with a McDonald's and a brazen office block of the Thatcher era . . . We are not, then, 'a mindless mob', but an international force against finance fetish and global enclosure for profit.[33]

Carnival's political thrust is converting humour and play into a subversive weapon that can challenge authority. In her book *Dancing in the Streets,* Barbara Ehrenreich describes the 'costumes, music, impromptu dancing and the sharing of food and drink . . . the immediate joy of solidarity, if only because, in the face of overwhelming state and corporate power, solidarity is their sole source of strength', and 'the urge to transform one's appearance, to dance outdoors, to mock the powerful and embrace perfect strangers is not easy to suppress'.[34] The more serious-minded and humourless the target, the greater the potential to disrupt and challenge. With 'greedy' bankers in mind, Occupy Wall Street demonstrators have draped themselves in the American flag with dollar bills taped across their mouths. Others have cut to the chase with the slogan 'One day the poor will have nothing left to eat but the rich.' The tough policing of demonstrations has occasioned disarming responses – from the spontaneous embracing of police officers to bombarding them with over-sized teddy bears launched from a mega catapult.[35]

Culture Jammers

There is a long tradition of culture jamming in artwork and graffiti, but since the late 1980s it has been associated with assaults on corporate images and claims – 'guerrilla semiotics'. Culture jammers alter corporate logos and advertisements, spoof corporate statements and promote anti-advertisements, or 'subvertisements'. Culture jammers' basic unit of protest is the meme, the core unit of cultural transmission – visual, verbal or musical. They play on memes in their subvertisements to reproduce the style and format of the original advertisement or logo, but with a twist that derides the message: 'Obesity King', 'Stealbucks Coffee', 'Kentucky Fried Cruelty', 'Murder King', 'Frankenbucks', 'Chase Morally Bankrupt'.

Culture jammers' philosophy is, like that of carnival protestors, liberationist. They believe that by interrupting the ubiquitous consumption messages that define our wants and needs we are better able to question them and, should we choose, resist them. Adbusters, for example, has been a major player in the culture jamming business since the early 2000s. Its Buy Nothing Days urge us to 'take a global holiday from consumerism'. It specializes in anti-corporate campaigns and subvertisments sourced from 'a global network of artists, activists, writers, pranksters, students and entrepreneurs'.[36] It confronts some of the biggest brands with reworked advertisements and images that aim to startle and provoke an alternative reading, such as portraying Absolut vodka as 'Absolut Impotence' and parodying Calvin Klein's 'Obsession' perfume range with an image of a bulimic woman leaning over a toilet bowl. Other culture jammers include Negativland, a collective that confronts corporate culture with art and experimental music; Subvertise, a web gallery of subvertisements; and Memefest, which aspires to 'generate and release helpful memes which may bring some balance back into a brand-crazy world'. Effective subvertisements are able to seize attention at two levels: the conventional product, and its radical critique or challenge.

A variation on the subvertisement theme is billboard liberation, represented by the Billboard Liberation Front. Armed with aerosols and tins of paint, billboard liberationists judiciously adjust billboard messages in hit-and-run escapades. Examples include adding 'profit' beneath 'Love' on Coca-Cola billboards, and changing NatWest bank's 'Find out why millions of people across Britain save with us', to 'Find out why millions of people across Britain are unemployed with us'.

Some culture jammers favour media hoaxes, a speciality of The Yes Men. They claim to impersonate 'big-time criminals in order to publicly humiliate them, and otherwise [give] journalists excuses to cover important issues'.[37] Posing as spokespersons for 'the criminals' – major companies – they have appeared on news channels, websites and YouTube videos, and addressed major conferences. Their carefully choreographed ruses are invariably plausible, designed to expose and embarrass their corporate victims. On 3 December 2004, the twentieth anniversary of Union Carbide's Bhopal disaster, one of the Yes Men posed as a representative of Dow Chemical, the company that had purchased Union Carbide. He announced on the BBC World Service that his company would finally take full responsibility for the medical care and compensation of the many victims of the Bhopal industrial disaster of 1984, something that they had long resisted.[38] The declaration forced Dow executives into a rapid and vociferous denial which, for a short while, wiped $2 billion off the company's share value.[39]

A final feature of culture jamming is droplifting, or shop-dropping – the surreptitious leaving of things in shops. Artists and musicians have long been known to droplift their work to get free promotion, but politicized droplifting makes a rather different point: the questionable credentials of the product on sale. One approach has been to add genuine-looking stickers to products on the shop shelves, such as 'Now with appetite suppressants' on packages of factory-farmed beef, and 'More phosphate than any other brand' to bottles of Diet Coke.

How might we judge culture jamming? Dagny Nome reflects on this question:

Walking down the street I pass a Nike poster. I hardly notice it, living in the city I am surrounded by commercial messages. But something is not right with this one. I look again. What happened to the usual black athlete? Why is there a woman carrying a child, in exactly the same pose as the athlete occupied in the posters I'd already seen? And the text – it describes working conditions in Indonesian factories where Nike shoes are made. The final message is 'so think globally before you decide it's so cool to wear Nike'. It is clearly not an ad sponsored by Nike, yet the visual layout seems the same. That is why I at first thought it was an ad for Nike, and mentally approached it that way. And that is why the negative message surprises me, and ultimately, why I will remember it.[40]

Culture jamming is innovative in its methods and a small thorn in the side of big business, creatively using advertisers' techniques against them and their clients. Moreover it has the air of serious fun, something to smile about but also to ponder. Culture jammers are among the foot soldiers of confrontational politics and, like radical social pressure groups, clear in their position: their target is unquestionably bad, exploitative or misleading – which can provoke an equal and opposite reaction from those they attack. For instance, the advertising industry has begun to adopt the irony that culture jammers use, but to their clients' advantage. Beyond occasional news reports, no culture jammer has yet been able to obtain promotion time on commercial TV channels; they are threats to the channel's core income stream. Naomi Klein had it about right when she described culture jamming as 'more a drop in the bucket than a spanner in the works'.[41] It is unlikely to radically reconfigure capitalism or prevent over-varnished corporate claims; the 'beast' is not so easily cowed. But it is, perhaps, a little more wary.

Non-governmental Organizations

It is estimated that more than 40,000 non-governmental organizations (NGOs) operate internationally, and 52,000 nationally.[42] NGOs can move with alacrity in areas where establishment officials are cautious or absent, especially on issues such as human rights, peace and poverty. NGO agitation and agenda-setting has helped achieve some historic milestones, contributing to the abolition of slavery back in the 1800s (the Anti-slavery Society) and, in the twentieth century, the outlawing of landmines in conventional warfare (the International Campaign to Ban Landmines).

NGOs are often portrayed as a corrective to the limitations and dysfunctions of state institutions and the market. They attract people who are frustrated by conventional avenues of social influence. Professionalized NGOs such as Greenpeace, Oxfam, Shelter, Médecins Sans Frontières and Save the Children offer a seemingly direct and transparent route to tackle urgent social problems; in effect, an alternative form of politics. As donors or participants, NGO members invest in an expertise and ideology they believe they can trust, and that can address issues that personally concern them.[43]

Pinning down exactly what makes an NGO an NGO is a vexing endeavour. In the late 1990s the United Nations – itself an NGO – ventured this 'authoritative', tortuous definition:

A non-profit entity whose members are citizens or associations of citizens of one or more countries and whose activities are determined by the collective will of its members in response to the needs of the members of one or more communities with which the NGO cooperates.[44]

In these terms, any group that is not a private, for profit organization can qualify for NGO status. The definition is ethically neutral so, in principle, no cause is excluded, such as the National Rifle Association, the leading pro-firearm NGO that has consultative status at the UN.

A more nuanced definition is submitted by Professor Peter Willetts of City University, London:

> The groups may vary in size from mass organizations that mobilize large segments of society to small numbers of people. They may speak on behalf of the poor and oppressed or they may represent privileged elites. They may engage in advocacy; run operational programmes; provide a great variety of public services; promote and sustain many types of social, economic, and political cooperation; or raise funds for other organizations to spend.[45]

NGOs vary in their style of operation. Some rely on working partnerships and aim for 'win-win' outcomes. The World Wide Fund for Nature (WWF) has partnered with Unilever on sustainable fisheries; the World Resources Institute joined with British Petroleum, General Motors and Monsanto to develop policies on sustainable development and climate change; and the Environmental Defense Fund has collaborated with landowners and the U.S. Fish and Wildlife Service to work towards restoring local wildlife habitat. But these arrangements are not without risk for the NGO – of corporate capture. An NGO negotiator explains:

> When you get into these dialogues, of course what you get is an army of corporate lawyers come through the door with, you know, 58 other senior executives and you have two people

sat on your side of the desk and that's where on occasions you get this suspicion that . . . we can string this out for as long as you want because we have got people here who can come in, whilst we get on with our business.[46]

The risk of capture increases when an NGO accepts corporate donations – because it needs to. Some NGOs' annual budgets for projects, salaries and overheads run to millions of dollars, so they seek funding from various sources, including private-sector companies. A number of NGOs rely on governmental contributions to maintain their operations, the position of Oxfam, Médecins Sans Frontières and the WWF. None of these arrangements means that their key goals are necessarily compromised, but they can be perceived as such.

In contrast, there are NGOs that are firm about not confusing the boundaries between 'us' and 'them' in their philosophy or funding. They are in the confrontation-and-blame business. Earth First! is a prime example. Its website asserts its position in unequivocal terms:

Are you tired of namby-pamby environmental groups? Are you tired of overpaid corporate environmentalists who suck up to bureaucrats and industry? Have you become disempowered by the reductionist approach of environmental professionals and scientists? . . . If you answered yes to any of these questions, then Earth First! is for you. Earth First! is effective. Our front-line, direct action approach to protecting wilderness gets results.[47]

Earth First! prides itself on its anarchic, 'no members' character, and describes itself as a diverse population, 'from animal rights vegans to wilderness hunting guides, from shrill voices to careful followers of Gandhi, from whiskey-drinking backwoods riffraff to thoughtful philosophers, from misanthropes to humanists'.[48] It is wedded to high-visibility adversarial action of the sort long favoured by Greenpeace, who are adept at breathtaking confrontations. Greenpeace's Brent Spar operation in 1995 was a watershed – literally and figuratively – in this respect.

Brent Spar was a large, abandoned oil storage buoy anchored in the North Sea, owned by Shell. With agreement of the UK government, Shell planned to tow the buoy into the Atlantic and sink it. Shell claimed it was the best environmental option, a view endorsed by some independent experts. Others, however, were concerned about the toxicity of the remaining waste aboard the buoy.[49] Greenpeace shared these worries but were just as anxious about ethical issues. As they saw it, the seas should not be seen as a convenient dumping ground for industrial waste.

Greenpeace activists drew attention to their cause by boarding Brent Spar and holing up there. But, following a lively confrontation with Shell security staff, they were forcibly ejected. Meanwhile, dramatic television coverage of the occupation was beamed across the globe; the event was international news and triggered a boycott of some of Shell's filling stations. Greenpeace then decided to reoccupy Brent Spar, which provoked a sea battle worthy of a Hollywood production, with Shell boarding parties swinging into action and wrestling with the few activists aboard. Eventually, in the face of mounting international pressure and damaging public relations for Shell, Shell backed down, ceding victory to Greenpeace.

Brent Spar was eventually towed to land and dismantled. A casualty of the campaign was some of the truth – the actual amount of toxic waste remaining was found to be far less than Greenpeace had claimed, which did not help Greenpeace's standing. But Shell was also stung by the event and forced to radically review its environmental policies, as well as its rules of engagement with NGOs and the wider public.[50]

NGO confrontations with their quarry have grown in sophistication over the years, and are not just of the physically grappling sort. They include disrupting a target's communication network and influencing its stakeholders – investors, suppliers, financial backers. Shareholder meetings are a favourite, where an NGO can lodge a resolution critical of corporate policy or governance. Corporate social media channels and websites have been sabotaged and Facebook used to build a virtual community of protestors. The enrolment of prominent celebrities to an NGO's cause can bring instant media attention.

But there are many NGOs that prefer backstage influence to front-stage confrontation. Public Citizen, founded by Ralph Nader in the 1970s, is committed to defending consumer rights and ensuring that 'all citizens are represented in the halls of power'.[51] It engages in intense lobbying and petitioning of government on matters such as health and environmental protection. CorpWatch scrutinizes corporate ethical conduct and publicizes its findings in articles and on its website. It takes credit for exposing the poor condition of Nike's workers in Vietnam in the 1990s. Global Witness aims to tackle the 'resource curse', where governments and companies aggressively exploit natural resources in ways that exacerbate conflict, corruption and human rights abuses. They utilize in-depth investigations and case studies to advocate for policy change.

There is now a network of citizen-actors who hold organizations and administrations to account. The community grows as social injustices become more apparent and economic systems fail to provide fairly for everyone. From the quirky and idiosyncratic to the long-standing and highly professional, these groups have become fundamental to a pluralistic society and democratic accountability. We may not agree with all of their aims and methods, but we would probably be much poorer without them.

5

The Empires Strike Back

In 1999 New Zealand experienced its own 'WikiLeaks' moment – a rare exposure of the behind-the-scenes workings of a corporate campaign against activists.

It hinged upon the lucrative logging of the ancient rainforests on the West Coast. The forests were publicly owned and managed by the state's timber production company, Timberlands West Coast Ltd. The company's official line was that its logging was highly selective and caused minimal ecological damage. But environmental activists, under the umbrella of the Native Forest Action Committee, saw things differently. The logging was unnecessary and inappropriate; it was a desecration of a primordial forest that harboured native wildlife; the habitat had to be protected. The activists publicized their concerns in dramatic forest confrontations and anti-Timberlands graffiti. The local press was alive to the drama and reported Timberlands in none too flattering terms. Timberlands, fearful of losing the public relations battle, hired four public relations firms to put their case and counter the clamour – three local firms and one international one, Shandwick, now Weber Shandwick.

The dispute might have faded from public view were it not for the actions of a whistle-blower inside Timberlands concerned about the methods the organization was using in its public relations campaign. The whistle-blower chose to leak a large dossier of confidential documents to an investigative journalist, which formed the substance of a book, *Secrets and Lies* by Nicky Hager and Bob Burton.[1] The 288-page volume appears solidly researched and reproduces many of the source documents as evidence, as well as freedom of information data. We learn how Timberlands' executives set out to 'neutralize'a full range of critics of logging, including environmental groups, members of parliament and environmental scientists. Their strategy involved 'collecting information on individuals, sending public relations staff and others to conservation meetings incognito and arranging for fake approaches to environmental groups to gather information'.[2] Other assertions include:

Shandwick drafting pro-Timberlands letters to be sent off to newspapers' editors to complain about journalists who wrote articles critical of the company.[3]

Shandwick seeking the 'dirt' on Timberlands' critics and targeting pro-environmental celebrities such as Anita Roddick of The Body Shop.[4]

Shandwick quietly creating an 'independent' pro-logging community group to counter the activists' claims.[5]

Timberlands' staff, in police-intelligence style, photographing and videoing protestors and sending the images off to Shandwick 'to show them what we're up against'.[6]

Timberlands' lawyers issuing legal warnings to those who obstructed logging, with threats of considerable fines.[7]

Shandwick is described as growing progressively more desperate, at one time drafting a letter of objection for Timberlands addressed to the schools' principals – because pupils had joined a protest outside Parliament against Timberlands' operations.[8] Yet, despite all these efforts, the protests continued and support grew for the protection of the forests. Timberlands was especially stung by bad publicity after one of its logging helicopters destroyed an activist's treetop platform, using a suspended log as a battering ram. It happened just as a protester was preparing to climb the tree; she was terrified.[9]

The end of the affair was messy for Shandwick, with an investigation into its practices by the Public Relations Institute, an overseeing body of the profession.[10] Meanwhile, the incoming administration in New Zealand vetoed Timberlands' scheme, and all native timber milling on the West Coast was halted. Timberlands ceased trading in 2008.

The Public Relations of Public Relations

The Timberlands-Shandwick story reveals public relations at work at the behest of a well-resourced client, and some of the tools of the public relations trade – their use and abuse. Public relations is a potent means for an organization to project the image it wants for itself and to defend itself from adverse criticism. Not all campaigns are as questionable as Shandwick's, but, mindful of such incidents, the profession takes pains to declare that 'fairness and openness' is central to its practice.[11] Public relations expertise can be found in most large companies and independent agencies, some focusing on 'crisis management' and 'reputation recovery'.

Front Groups

The roots of public relations can be traced to the pioneering work of Edward Louis Bernays in the 1950s. Bernays was convinced that 'intelligent manipulation', as he put it, was an essential ingredient of a democratic society,[12] and he led the way in the use of front groups – organizations that have the sole mission of advancing the interests of the enterprises that fund them and overcoming resistance to their sponsor's goals. Bernays was noted for setting up more institutes and foundations than Rockefeller and Carnegie combined, each designed to publicize information that supported its client's aims.[13] For example, his way of helping the U.S. trucking industry obtain more money from Congress for new highways was to create the Trucking Information Service, Trucking Service Bureau and the Better Living Through Increased Highway Transportation group.

Corporations create front groups to influence legislators, the media and consumers. Front groups are able to generate a stream of press releases, 'breakthroughs' and video clips that fall into news reporters' laps and provide them with instant, authoritative-looking copy. Front-group spokespersons appear on talk shows, hold conferences and publish newsletters. According to the Center for Media and Democracy, in 2013 there were at least 190 front groups across North America, Europe, the UK and Australia.[14]

It is often difficult to distinguish a front group from a genuine, independent, information or research centre – which, of course, is the general idea. The illusion is created through labels and titles that give the impression of an authoritative, disinterested party – 'astroturfing', after AstroTurf carpeting designed to look like real grass. Disinformation is easier to believe if it comes from a seemingly disinterested party, but clues that the group may not be all it appears are when it frequently mentions its 'prestigious experts', when it avoids mentioning its funding sources or, more blatantly, when its name does not appear to correspond to what it actually does. The purview of front groups is broad. For example:

- Protect the Harvest states that its purpose is 'to fight back and defend American families, farmers, hunters and animal owners from the growing threat posed by the radical animal rights movement'. It is underwritten by the Lucas Cattle and Lucas Oil Companies in the U.S.[15]

- Energy in Depth was formed by the multi-billion-dollar petroleum and gas industry and a public relations firm to provide 'research' and 'fact sheets' that support fracking, and to argue against regulatory controls.[16]

- The International Food Information Council states its mission is 'to effectively communicate science-based information about food safety and nutrition to health professionals, government officials, educators, journalists, and consumers'.[17] Its main supporters are leading food, pesticide and biotech companies including Kraft, McDonald's, Nestlé, Monsanto and Dupont.[18]

- Wise Use advocates a free-market approach to environmental protection and the opening of public lands to mining and energy production, including the Arctic National Wildlife Refuge in Alaska.[19] It receives most of its support from resource-extraction industries.[20]

- The Center for Consumer Freedom raises the banner of civil liberties and 'protecting consumer choice'. Funding is mainly from food companies, but the Center prefers not to disclose precisely which, 'in light of violence and of the forms of aggression from activists'.[21] It hosts 'market freedom' projects such as ActivistCash.com dedicated to countering NGO 'radical agendas', like Adbusters': 'Imagine a world without McDonald's, Nike, or Kraft Foods. A world where the budget-conscious and time-strapped have nowhere to grab a quick bite, where almost no one drives a car, where television is extinct. Sounds pretty bleak? This is the utopian vision of the Adbusters Media Foundation.'[22]

Anti-activism

Anti-activism, as the Timberlands case shows, is a strand of public relations activity. It is backed up by practitioner texts that include Denise Deegan's *Managing Activism* and Keva Silversmith's *A pr Guide to Activist Groups*.[23] These purport to give 'the inside facts' on social activism and advise practitioners on how to respond to different types of activists. The books' language is often militaristic: 'get to know the enemy'; 'think like an activist'; 'deal with hostile groups'; 'respond effectively to a mass social media attack'; 'when to fight'; and 'how to fight'. The 'enemy' may appear 'irrational' or 'emotional', but has to be coolly appraised. Simply ignoring it is not recommended. Deegan makes the point with stories about companies that did just that and paid the price, such as Nike.

In the world of public relations, Nike stands as a textbook example of how corporations should not deal with activists. In 1996 Nike was targeted by campaigners about its alleged sweatshop conditions and mistreatment of workers in Asia. Nike's response was to distance itself from the accusation. It argued that the problem was not theirs but rested with their Asian subcontractors, over whom they had no direct control. This simply fanned the flames of protest, culminating in a CBS television documentary that portrayed cowed Nike workers and evasive managers.

Soon other news media took up the story and the assault on Nike's human rights record moved into high gear. Nike reacted by powering up its public relations and issuing a barrage of press releases, advertisements, pamphlets and letters to newspapers to reassure the public that everything was now legal and above board. These claims were met with suspicion by Nike's critics and, after two years of sustained pressure, Nike finally changed tack and agreed to increase the accountability of its subcontractors and require u.s. working and educational standards of its contracted labour.

Corporate Spooks

Public relations' formal mandate is to present a product, service or project honestly and in the best possible light. But, unofficially, public relations advantage can be gained by outmanoeuvring a critic or opponent with information obtained surreptitiously.

It is difficult to judge the extent of clandestine public relations, hardly the stuff of company annual reports, and effective spies, by definition, are not detected. The occasional revelation, such as the Timberlands case, suggests there may be more than meets the eye. Cara Shaffer is another example. In 2007, posing as student, she contacted the Student/Farmworker Alliance in Florida. She was eager to join their campaign to achieve fair treatment for Florida migrant workers who harvested tomatoes for Burger King and other fast-food chains.[24] Her insistent inquisitiveness in planning sessions raised suspicions, so they investigated her background. It transpired that she was the owner of a private security firm hired by Burger King to 'protect its employees and assets from potential harm'.[25] Her exposure coincided with an Internet smear campaign aimed at the Student/ Farmworker Alliance, also allegedly engineered by Burger King. Widespread media coverage resulted in a climb-down by Burger King, some dismissals and an 'internal investigation'.[26] A third example focuses on Dow Chemical, the victim of the Yes Men hoax that Dow was to compensate Bhopal victims (described in chapter Four). Emails released by the WikiLeaks organization revealed that, in response, Dow had hired a 'global intelligence' company to secretly monitor all Yes Men activities.[27]

More generally, private surveillance firms are said to be doing rather well in an increasingly competitive and paranoid global economy – 'Spies are sometimes the only people who can solve a company's problems', opines an executive of a major public relations/intelligence firm, and they make up around a quarter of the business.[28] John Stauber and Sheldon Rampton describe how, on the surface, many of these operations appear mundane:

> Have you ever wondered what it's like to talk to a [PR] spy? The field operatives . . . are typically polite, low-key and do their best to sound sympathetic to the people they are interrogating. They have misrepresented themselves, claiming falsely to be journalists, friends of friends, or supporters of social change. Most of the time, however, they simply give very limited information, identifying their company only by its initials and describing [it] euphemistically as a 'research group' which helps 'corporate decision makers . . . develop a better appreciation of the public interest movement' in order to 'resolve contentious public policy issues in a balanced and socially responsible manner'.[29]

Corporate Social Responsibility

Corporate social responsibility tackles blame differently. With a corporate social responsibility policy in place an organization aims to anticipate and forestall its critics. It is rare now to find a major company without a statement of social responsibility that claims interaction with stakeholders, contribution to a cleaner, more sustainable environment, and ethical conduct that exceeds legal obligations.

Since the 1990s 'the triple bottom line' has defined many such aspirations. The basic idea is that corporate profits – the traditional bottom line – should stand equally alongside two other bottom lines: care for people and planetary stewardship.[30] There are companies that have staked their reputation on it. In 2007, for example, Marks & Spencer announced a broad-ranging social responsibility 'Plan A with no Plan B'. Accreditation agencies add a degree of quality assurance, such as the European Eco-management and Audit Scheme (EMAS), the

International Organization for Standardization, Fair Trade and the Global Reporting Initiative. Each determines criteria of social stewardship, as well as the fees required for membership and certification.

There have been attempts to rank different companies on their socially responsible performance, a challenging task given the vast spectrum of organizations, the variability of available information and the mix of criteria. One of the more rigorous classifications is produced annually by Corporate Knights, a Toronto-based research company. It examines companies over a range of major social and sustainability indices, including their approach to energy usage, carbon emissions, water conservation and staff incentives for 'clean capitalism'.[31] In 2012 Northern European and UK companies outranked U.S. companies. The Danish pharmaceutical firm, Novo Nordisk, commanded the top spot with, it was judged, sustainability rooted deeply in its working culture. Companies that did poorly tended to pay lip service to social responsibility, more image than substance.

Raising the Green Flag

Once a company hoists the flag of corporate social responsibility, it also raises public expectations that it means it. Social responsibility is a double-edged sword. It attracts praise when it is honestly delivered and derision if it turns out to be an empty promise. For example, consider the following declaration from BP, published in *Our Code: It's What We Believe*:

> We want to make a positive difference wherever we do business. We hold ourselves to the highest ethical standards and behave in ways which earn the trust of communities in which we operate. We work hard to create open and sincere relationships with local communities, as well as with bodies such as nongovernmental organizations (NGOs) who have a legitimate interest in what we do as a company. We respect

the rights and dignity of communities, NGOs and other organizations with whom we interact.[32]

The events of 20 April 2010 tested this to near breaking point, when BP's Deepwater Horizon oil well exploded, killing eleven workers. The blast created the biggest offshore spill in U.S. history: some 1,000 miles (1,600 km) of the Gulf of Mexico shoreline was polluted from 200 million gallons (760 million litres) of crude oil, devastating local fisheries and the livelihoods of those who depended on them. BP's reputation plummeted. It was blamed for lax safety procedures and for putting profits before safety and the environment. The infamous apology of its chief executive did not help: 'We're sorry for the massive disruption it's caused, there's no one who wants this thing over more than I do, I'd like my life back.'

Ford Motor Company was another instance. In 2005 its annual sustainability report contained the announcement that it would produce 250,000 hybrid vehicles by 2010. The pledge was warmly received by environmentalists. But by mid-2006 Ford reneged on its commitment; it looked a much poorer business investment than they had anticipated. The response from environmental NGOs was excoriating. They took out full-page advertisements accusing the company of breaking its promise on fuel economy, under the strapline: 'Ford still makes America's worst gas guzzlers. Don't buy Bill Ford's environmental promises. Don't buy his cars.'[33]

Deflection

Some firms – producers of weapons, manufacturers of tobacco products, purveyors of 'junk' food, exploiters of rainforests, aggressive trawler fishers – have an uphill struggle convincing their critics that they are socially responsible. Unsurprisingly, their corporate social responsibility statements are often evasive or elliptical about the social ramifications of their business.

British American Tobacco, for instance, skirts around health issues, stressing that the issue is 'about consumer choice', and that it is better that a 'responsible' employer like them meets the demand. There is no mention of how the company stimulates the demand for tobacco.[34] But all is not lost for socially tainted companies. They can deflect attention from what they actually do by attaching their name to something generally perceived as wholesome or desirable – a good cause or a non-profit organization; they can garner credit by proxy. If public attitudes towards a firm or industry can be softened by the judicious distribution of corporate monies, it is harder for activists to reach sympathetic audiences and make their challenges stick. Some illustrations:

- In the late twentieth century, U.S. tobacco companies sponsored over 2,700 programmes and events, ranging from AIDS awareness and education to arts and minorities, at a cost of $365 million.[35] Before European and U.S. legislation outlawing the practice, cigarette brands were commonly associated with sports such as motor racing, snooker, tennis and rugby.

- The Italian weapons firm Finmeccanica became a corporate sponsor of London's National Gallery in 2011 – but ended its association a year later following protests from artists and campaigners.[36]

- American arms manufacturers gave the National Rifle Association nearly $40 million between 2005 and 2012.[37] The National Rifle Association is, in the eyes of some 50 per cent of the U.S. population, an unquestionably good cause.

The arts, sport and health charities are common beneficiaries, as are universities and independent research centres.[38] Professor Ian Roberts of the London School of Hygiene and Tropical Medicine gives us a glimpse of its micro-politics.[39] He describes how a powerful triumvirate of Coca-Cola executives cornered him at a World Health Organization meeting on health and climate change. They were keen to fund research on how to get people more physically active: was he interested? 'It is not surprising', writes Roberts, 'that a company selling an energy-dense soft drink might want to focus attention on the output side of the personal energy-balance equation. It would be more convenient to lay the blame for population fatness on a lack of cycle paths than on the 35g of sugar contained in a 330ml Coke can.' In response, Roberts suggested to Coca-Cola an alternative project: an investigation into the road deaths and injuries associated with Coca-Cola's road-distribution network and the impacts of the fossil fuels they used on climate change. He heard no more from the company: 'I am sure that Coca-Cola will find other universities eager to pluck the low-hanging fruit of industry-sponsored research', he mused. 'If my experience is anything to go by, not much plucking will be necessary.'

Roberts's experience touches on the more general way in which some sectors of the market have presented themselves as complementary to social responsibility, rather than antagonistic to it. In these terms, big profits can be made, but then recirculated among deserving causes. Some extremely rich entrepreneurs, such as Bill Gates of Microsoft, financial speculator George Soros and the founders of Google, have adopted this approach. They are widely portrayed as ethical people doing something positive about world problems. Corporations such as Coca-Cola, Starbucks and Costa Coffee have incorporated ethical sourcing into their marketing to give the impression that when we purchase their drinks we are also purchasing a stake in doing good.

These efforts divide critics. For some they represent capitalism at its best. For others they are seen as propping up or green-washing a fundamentally flawed system. Philosopher Slavoj Žižek, for instance, argues that when exploitation and damage is patched up with the same wealth it creates, it does no more than perpetuate the core problem – the original market system. It needs replacing.[40]

My Enemy is Now My Friend

Strategic partnerships, intersectoral partnerships, social alliances, cross-sectoral dialogues – these are all terms used to describe collaborative relationships between corporations and non-profit organizations. The scene switches from mutual recrimination to pragmatic appreciation.

The incentives for a corporation to enter into a partnership may be reactive or proactive: reactive from battle weariness with an intimidating adversary; proactive from recognition that there are gaps in their expertise that can best be filled by some NGOs. Indeed, in developing countries NGOs are often the only reliable source of information about local needs. The World Bank, for example, extensively solicits NGO knowledge and support in the design of its international development projects. Similarly, pharmaceutical companies that supply key medicines cheaply to developing countries have fostered partnerships with the World Health Organization and Médecins Sans Frontières to help them decide where best to target and distribute their drugs.

A partnership with a grassroots NGO can give a company a fresh view of shifts in society to build into their long-term business plans. It can also help solve a local problem. For example, mining companies in Katanga in the Democratic Republic of Congo operate on land that is also mined, illegally, by many artisanal workers – women and children who literally scrape a living, panning for minerals and burrowing in unstable underground excavations. The work is unregulated and extremely hazardous. Rather than attempt to expel them, companies have partnered with NGOs committed to creating alternatives for the workers, providing them with skills-training and micro credit for small businesses.[41]

Corporate–NGO partnerships are important alternatives to conflictual, blame-centred relationships, but they should not be over-idealized; they do not eliminate the contest for control. From the company's perspective some partnerships are easier to manage than others, especially those that are at arm's length. They may give the company greater opportunity to determine the ground rules. In contrast, a closer relationship offers the possibility of a different kind of control: the capturing of an old adversary in the hope of de-radicalizing their demands and forestalling future blame scenarios.

6

Blame Government

As a rule, private businesses deal with blame defensively, protecting their own and their shareholders' interests. But public-sector organizations, as the name suggests, look to a much wider constituency. Public agencies, government members and civil servants are expected to account openly for what they do with public money and justify their decisions and actions. This is a key strand of governance in a modern democracy that requires clear channels of credit and blame, clarity about who is responsible for what, and sanctions if things go wrong.

The size and scope of the public sector vary between nations, reflecting their histories and ideologies. The largest are to be found in Denmark and Norway, comprising 30 per cent of the workforce; the smallest are in Korea and Japan at around 6 per cent. The u.s. and uk are in between, at 16 and 19 per cent respectively.[1] Publicly funded services cover a plethora of activities – health, ageing, defence, animal inspection, prison, foreign affairs, transport, education, energy, refugees, social security and taxation, to name but a few. Some functions may be outsourced to private business, blurring the boundaries of accountability.

Blame Games

Governments get blamed when their structures are unwieldy, their offices rule-obsessed or obstructive or when their policies clearly make things worse. This is ammunition for point-scoring in the blame games of party politics, especially by exaggerating an opponent's failures. Blame-avoidance strategies are common when governments defend their reputations, particularly on matters over which they have little or no control.

A major difficulty for politicians is negative bias. There is now considerable evidence that electorates are more attuned to what they have lost from a particular politician or party than what they have gained; that is what sticks in their mind when they vote. It is wiser, then, not to concentrate exclusively on trumpeting one's achievements; softening or mitigating the downsides of a policy or action is just as important. The point is illustrated in a little experiment by Georg Wenzelburger of the University of Freiburg.[2] He presented two groups of students with a fictitious but authentic-looking newspaper article about the Canadian government cutting social benefits by 15 per cent – ostensibly a vote-loser among many citizens. However, the details of the stories differed between the groups. One identified the cuts and outlined the facts about how it positively affected the budget balance and helped stimulate economic growth. The second added several blame-avoidance caveats: the prime minister was forced into the measure because of the global financial crisis; the opposition and unions had been consulted; and mechanisms would be put in place to manage debt-reduction more progressively in the future. After reading the reports the students were asked what they thought about the austerity measures and the Canadian prime minister. Those who had read the blame-avoidance accounts were the most supportive of the austerity move and the prime minister.

Governments, Wenzelburger concludes, would do well to use blame avoidance in their communications. And many do just that: policy failures are not failures but the result of unforeseen circumstances/opposition sabotage/world events/obstructive unions/an ineffective state agency and so forth. These, according to Professor Christopher Hood of Oxford University, are examples of presentational strategies. He discerns a structure to them, encapsulated in four dictums: 'Divert the attention of your critics or the public'; 'Keep your head down until it blows over'; 'Fight your corner to win over your audience'; and 'Disarm your critics before they turn nasty.'[3] Spinning information – turning negatives into positives and blame into credit, ensuring others interpret events in ways that minimize reputational harm – is part of the process. In major crises the services of spin doctors may be required, experts in the art of bending facts and managing impressions without – quite – lying. A common ploy is to use statistics selectively to demonstrate a positive policy outcome, while ignoring information that indicates the opposite. Ambiguity means you cannot be pinned down, and speaking in euphemisms presents unpleasant or unwelcome news in a more palatable form. Some spin euphemisms are remarkable for their linguistic ingenuity. Former CIA chief David Petraeus apologized in March 2013 for 'slipping my moorings', alluding to his affair with his biographer. In Bill Clinton's presidential campaign he admitted he had smoked marijuana, but quickly added that he 'didn't inhale', to suggest he did not get high. Hillary Clinton claimed she did 'mis-speak' when she said she had been pinned down by sniper fire on a visit to Bosnia in 2008, but when video coverage indicated otherwise. And, since the 1980s, being 'economical with the truth' has been a favoured substitution for 'lying' among British politicians.[4]

Accountability and Blame

Public accountability and blameworthiness run in tandem, at times along labyrinthine channels. In parliamentary systems citizens confer responsibility to their elected representatives, who defer to a prime minister and cabinet. Cabinet ministers delegate powers to their civil servants who route political directives and resources to specialist agencies that provide services to individual citizens. This lengthy chain of accountability/blame, the 'Westminster model', is the system in the UK and the former British Commonwealth, as well as in Belgium, the Netherlands and Germany.

Unlike the parliamentary system, presidential systems separate the elected leader from the legislature, a system of 'checks and balances' designed to curtail abuse of power. In the U.S. the legislative body comprises two elected chambers, the House of Representatives that drafts bills and the Senate that ratifies them. Only after successful passage through both can bills be signed into law by the president. In theory this ensures democratic accountability, but who exactly to blame or praise becomes messier when the chambers are controlled by different political parties, or when they simply cannot see eye to eye. It happened with 'Obamacare', a landmark – but divisive – bill passed by the House of Representatives in 2010. It sought to bring affordable healthcare to millions of poorer Americans, but was fiercely resisted on ideological and economic grounds by all Republicans in the Senate, along with some Democrats. Amid acrimonious exchanges, raw partisanship, prejudices and 'kill the bill' demonstrations, Obama fought desperately to bring sufficient dissidents on board to achieve a majority, which he eventually did.

Many Hands

The actualities of government rarely fall neatly into the lines of accountability. It is common for many different people to contribute to particular decisions, making it difficult to identify exactly who should bear the brunt of blame when things go wrong, dubbed 'the problem of many hands'.[5] Governmental and public agency decisions unfold over time, across many different desks, committees and organizational levels, a diffusion of responsibilities that make it difficult to single out a blameworthy figure or figures.

There are, in principle, some ways around the problem. Blame may be apportioned by independent parties, an approach taken by congressional and parliamentary enquiries. Alternatively, there is the 'the buck stops here' response. It is said that U.S. President Harry Truman had just such a sign on his desk. The complexities of who did exactly what are sidestepped by the person at the top of the pyramid, who takes the blame. President John F. Kennedy defaulted to this position following the failure of the Bay of Pigs invasion in Cuba (while privately he blamed the CIA, the military Joint Chiefs of Staff and others). Public blame-taking of this sort is not the most comfortable position for political leaders who are, by definition, on the periphery of the complex apparatus of government. However it is appealing in its simplicity and can avert lengthy external investigations. Those below the chief are sheltered from the public eye but are likely to be subject to internal disciplinary review.

Many Eyes

As well as the many hands of public life, there are many eyes looking on. The media's gaze is relentless. Political commentary and the failings of public services are mainstays of daily news; politicians' utterances are pored over, especially their inconsistencies and idiosyncrasies. Intense media attention has become part and parcel of a politician's life, with a commensurate rise in the potential for blame: dubious or illegal work practices and unusual private-life preferences are hard to hide. Other lookers-on include official regulators and ombudsmen, charged with monitoring public agencies and ensuring public accountability. Professional bodies, too, are part of the accountability picture, in principle ensuring the ethical standards of their members. There are many different professions represented in public service, including police, doctors, teachers, social workers, engineers, judges, lawyers and dentists.

Just how well all these mechanisms work is a moot point. Professional associations are concerned with public relations and protecting their profession's interests, often more so than finding fault with their members. Resource-squeezed regulators can fail to pick up or respond to malpractice or mismanagement, notably during the financial crisis of 2008. The U.S. Securities and Exchange Commission, along with other regulators and overseers, did not spot the high-risk loan practices of the major banks. There are occasions when several lines of accountability fail, as occurred in the case of British doctor Harold Shipman. In 2000 he was jailed for killing fifteen of his patients over a number of years, and was suspected of murdering some 250 in all by injecting them with lethal doses of diamorphine. In a public inquiry the police were blamed for missed opportunities, the coroners for poor inspection of death certificates, the doctors' professional body for being too concerned with looking after its own, and the Home Office for not preventing his stockpiling of controlled drugs. Shipman gave no reasons for his actions and took his own life in jail.

Many eyes can also mean more reasons to *feel* blamed. Public accountability should ideally be a two-way street, a way for citizens to see how their money is spent and an opportunity for accountees to reflect on their practice and, if necessary, improve it. Rarely, however, is this the picture we get from those who face accountability demands. Robert Behn, in *Rethinking Democratic Accountability*, captures the mood:

> These accountability holdees have a very clear picture of what being held accountable means to them – to them personally. They recognize that, if someone is holding them accountable two things can happen. When they do something good, nothing happens. But when they screw up, all hell can break loose.[6]

Honourable Members

As public representatives, politicians stand for some of the loftier societal values such as truth, honesty and fairness. Some politicians go on record to declare the positive influence of their religious beliefs in these areas. However, in the rough and tumble of political life, and under the scrutiny of a critical press, espoused values soon get challenged and any deviations exposed; they are hostages to fortune.

Surveys tell us that politicians generally operate against a backdrop of public mistrust, aggravated in times of scandal – long woven into the trajectory of political life.[7] In the u.s. the first presidential sex scandal was Thomas Jefferson's purported affair with his slave Sally Hemming, some 200 years before Bill Clinton's 'improper physical relationship' with his intern Monica Lewinsky. Clinton was the second president to be impeached; the first was President Andrew Jackson in 1868 for 'high crimes and misdemeanours'. In recent years political scandal has soured the reputations of scores of politicians, including Ronald Reagan and Richard Nixon in the u.s.; Jeffrey Archer, Jeremy Thorpe and Neil Hamilton in the uk; and Silvio Berlusconi in Italy.

Moral errors and rule-bending are part and parcel of being human, but the bar is raised for politicians. The outrage about British mps' expenses is instructive in this respect. As 'honourable members', British mps historically have been able to make 'reasonable' demands on the public purse when they are away from home, including claims for a range of allowances, such as for running a second home if they live outside London and for items of furniture and food. In 2009 the *Daily Telegraph,* using Freedom of Information legislation, published details of these claims. Uproar followed. More than 50 mps had claimed for more than one property by regularly 'flipping' their second home, switching its designation to claim the allowance. Some had rented out their second home while still claiming the allowance; others had failed to pay capital gains tax or overclaimed for mortgages. The long list of additional claims ranged from the banal, such as garlic peelers, mugs and moth traps, to the extraordinary – adult movies, moat cleaning and duck house renovation. The system that ratified the claims came under fierce criticism, but the most ire was directed at those MPs who were seen to have abused their position of trust and forfeited their moral integrity.

Blame-mitigation excuses began to flow, from the bullish to the plaintive. Many were along the lines of 'I didn't break any rules', or 'it was what officials advised me to do', shifting the blame to 'the system'. 'It is clear that I was misled by the fees office into the arrangement in question', said one MP obliquely. Others were self-righteous: 'I've done nothing criminal . . . it's about jealousy' (millions of pounds spent on a private mansion); 'I believe this represents value for money for the taxpayer' (maintenance of his swimming pool); and 'I think people need to realize we are but human.' Recognizing the strength of public anger and the image damage, party leaders adopted a mea culpa position, apologizing on behalf of all politicians for the 'unethical claims' and promising radical reform. A number of MPs voluntarily repaid monies; others were directed to do so. There were resignations and several MPs were jailed for false accounting.

The crisis was a major tsunami for British politics. It hardened public disaffection with politicians as the government struggled to convince the public that the slate was now clean and abuses could no longer occur. The scandal can be seen as a victory for media scrutiny: the unearthing of unacceptable, hypocritical and illegal practices at the heart of government administration. But there is another, less newsworthy story to tell – that of stigmatizing the innocent. The worst cases came to represent the norm for all MPs despite the fact that, of the most inflammatory violations – second-home expenses – approximately half of all MPs were not implicated at all. Startling press headlines drew attention to the most flagrant abuses, accompanied by condemnatory comments. Thus, in the public eye, all politicians were soon to be construed as folk devils and ripe for demonization.

There is a paradox. Citizens in democracies regularly record their disenchantment with politicians' ruses, rhetorical tricks and broken promises; they can see through them. In the public eye politicians deserve the blame heaped upon them. Yet we are reluctant to throw out the baby, the party political system, with the political bathwater, the politicians.[8] An echo, perhaps, of Winston Churchill's observation: 'It has been said that democracy is the worst form of government except all those other forms that have been tried from time to time.' Maybe next time, next election, there will be fewer rotten apples, better leadership, more effective government, less need to blame. Maybe.

7

I'm Sorry

If someone is unjustly blamed, mistreated or victimized, an apology can help. It may not right a wrong, but it can start a process of healing and reconciliation. Yet apologies are perplexing. Why are we sometimes so reluctant to apologize? How do we know when apologies are genuine? And what is the significance of an institution apologizing – a government, state department or company – perhaps years after the event?

A Genuine Apology?

Apologies have different meanings depending on how they are expressed and the context. We can say sorry for someone's misfortune, an indication of sympathy. 'Sorry' can be used facetiously, suggesting that we do not really feel sorry at all. It can be a verbal reflex, something we say without thinking when we contravene social etiquette – bumping into a stranger, late arrival for an appointment. We may apologize to animals or even inanimate objects – the dead, a car or a plant.

There are also cultural dimensions. Anglo-American cultures prize individualism, competitiveness and winning, so apologizing can be a last-resort response. In collectivist cultures, such as Japan and China, apologies more often signal remorse and shame for disrupted harmony or social obligation. In Japan the individual becomes whole only when connected to the social unit (*jibun* is the word for self, meaning 'one's share of the shared life space').[1] For example, in 2010 the humble remorse of

Japan's prime minster, Yukio Hatoyama, was evident in a teary-eyed public apology announcing his resignation: 'The public has gradually refused to hear me. It's a shame and I'm solely to blame for it.'[2] When faced with extensive manufacturing problems in 2010 Toyota began vehicle recalls and promptly made public apologies, including full-page advertisements in Japanese and u.s. newspapers: 'We apologize from the bottom of our hearts for the great inconvenience and worries that we have caused you all.'[3] Contrast the response from the leaders of major u.s. investment banks for their role in the financial crises of 2007–2010 – a deafening silence: apologies were few and far between.

Apologies are especially meaningful when they address a moral injury or breach of trust. Here the apology usually demands more than just the words 'I'm sorry'; it should, according to psychologists, include an admission of personal failure, specificity about the nature of the offence, empathy (recognizing and feeling the victim's pain), unconditionality (no caveats, defensive clauses or vague generalities) and, if relevant, restitution or compensation. Unsurprisingly, few public apologies meet all of these conditions, although some get close. John Galliano, for example, was famous for his luxurious fashion designs as creative director of Christian Dior. In a Paris bar in 2010 it was alleged that he launched a drunken, anti-Semitic rant against two women, an outburst that cost him his job and reputation.[4] Shortly afterwards, he publicly apologized:

I fully accept that the accusations made against me have greatly shocked and upset people . . . I must take responsibility for the circumstances in which I found myself and for allowing myself to be seen to be behaving in the worst possible light. I only have myself to blame and I know that I must face up to my own failures and that I must work hard to gain people's understanding and compassion. To start this process I am seeking help and all I can hope for in time is to address the personal failure which led to these circumstances and try and earn people's forgiveness. Anti-Semitism and racism have no part in our society. I unreservedly apologise for my behaviour in causing any offence.[5]

And two years later he added:

I said and did things which hurt others, especially members of the Jewish community. I have expressed my sorrow privately and publicly for the pain which I caused, and I continue to do so.[6]

His case drew the attention of the u.s. Anti-Defamation League, which gave his remorse its stamp of approval, declaring that he had expressed 'true contrition' and had learned from his disgrace. The fashion world was cautiously prepared to accept him back.

The perceived genuineness of contrition often turns on the unspoken as much as the spoken – the handshake or hug to make amends, eye contact, tone of voice, facial expression – all closely scrutinized by the media when a public figure apologizes. For example, in 2013 Lance Armstrong, seven times winner of the Tour de France cycle race, appeared on Oprah Winfrey's television show. He solemnly admitted to a long history of taking performance-enhancing drugs, something he had denied adamantly for years. His act was an extraordinary about-face and mea culpa, yet not all observers were convinced. In the words of *Guardian* journalist Oliver Burkeman, it was 'a confession without confessing'. Burkeman added,

Bursting into tears during a conversation with Oprah may be corny, but appearing to be almost totally without emotion, as Armstrong did, is far worse. It draws the audience's attention to the fundamental falsity of the whole operation. You're supposed to leave the viewer feeling moved, and perhaps a little morally superior – not soiled for having tuned in at all.[7]

There are times when a spontaneous gesture of remorse can speak louder than any words, as German Chancellor Willy Brandt demonstrated in 1970. He was on a state visit to Poland where he attended a commemoration of the Jewish victims of the Warsaw Ghetto uprising of 1943, the last and fatal stand of some half a million corralled Jews, and a fraction of the six million who perished in the Holocaust. In a sombre, well-choreographed ceremony Brandt carefully laid a wreath at the memorial, but then startled onlookers by stepping back and kneeling down on the wet asphalt before the memorial. Head bowed and hands folded, he remained there in silence.

Writing afterwards about the incident he said: 'As I stood there at the bottom of the abyss of German history, under the burden of millions of victims of murder, I did what human beings do when speech fails them.'[8] For many people in Poland, the silent act was a powerful symbol of contrition for an over-whelming act of inhumanity; it was appreciated as a significant gesture of reconciliation. Yet it was received uneasily by the German people, who were preoccupied with the cultural pro-priety and meaning of such a blatant gesture by their leader. The cover of the German news weekly *Der Spiegel* featured a full-page image of Brandt kneeling at the monument, under the strapline 'Should Brandt Have Knelt?' Brandt, however, did not waver, and was later to reflect:

> Even twenty years later, I cannot say any more than the reporter whose account ran: 'Then he who does not need to kneel knelt, on behalf of all who do need to kneel but do not – because they dare not, or cannot, or cannot dare to kneel.'[9]

Brandt's solemn gesture contrasts with that of the Revd John Plummer. In November 1996 he was at a memorial meeting of

Vietnam War veterans in Washington. Present at the gathering was Phan Thi Kim Phuc, the subject of the Pulitzer Prize-winning photo of a young girl fleeing naked in despair from her village in Vietnam after an American napalm attack. Two of her brothers died in the same assault. Plummer described his feelings when he saw her at the meeting:

> I began to shake all over as wracking sobs were torn from my body. I felt like I was going to scream at the revelation that not only was I responsible for Kim's burns but that I had also killed her two brothers. She saw my grief, my pain, my sorrow. She held out her arms to me and embraced me. All I could say was 'I'm sorry; I'm so sorry; I'm sorry', over and over again. At the same time she was saying, 'It's all right, it's all right, I forgive; I forgive.'[10]

Plummer's guilt was rooted in his responsibility for sending napalm bombs into her village. It was he, he said, who had ordered the attack. It had tortured him for many years, but after Phan Thi Kim Phuc's forgiveness he at last felt at peace. His uncontrollable display of grief and contrition was heartfelt, but there was an unusual twist to the tale: he did not order the bombing raid. He was, according to the regional u.s. commander of the time, just a 'handyman' for the operations chief and had no authority to authorize flights.[11] Quizzed some months later on this discordant note, Plummer said that it was not his intention to deceive, but he felt deeply involved in the process and attached to the event of that day, along with a 'tremendous remorse that a little girl was hurt in something I was involved in, remote as it may be'. In effect, he felt *as if* he had pulled the lever to release the bombs and was therefore blameworthy.

Remorse and Justice

In the court of public opinion, the media, lack of remorse from a criminal offender is often taken as proof of their wayward or 'evil' character. Condemnatory headlines – 'Cold-blooded killer who has shown no remorse', 'No remorse shown in bicyclist's death', 'He showed no remorse and bragged about beating' – denounce offenders for what they did as well as for not apologizing: they are doubly guilty. In a similar vein, apologies are often factored into legal sentencing. American courts consider a defendant's expression of 'genuine remorse' in their recommendations, and in the UK judges may reduce a sentence if there is evidence of contrition. For example, in 2013 Judge Nigel Sweeney made the following remarks when sentencing two public figures for perverting the course of justice:

> *To defendant A*: I make clear that your lies and your endeavour to manipulate the process of the court will not add a day to your sentence, although they are likely in due course be relevant to the issue of costs. In any event you must receive a discount of 10 per cent to reflect the fact that your late plea [of guilty] took a degree of courage, saved the time and expense of a trial, and may reflect the beginnings of a degree of remorse – albeit that it is easy now to apologise for your wrongdoing.

> *To defendant B*: In my view the matters advanced on your behalf do not amount to exceptional circumstances, thus it is clear that an immediate custodial sentence must be imposed in your case as well. There can be no discount for a plea, nor is any for genuine remorse – clearly there is none.[12]

Remorse is strong currency in the courtroom, well known to defence attorneys. If a client is likely to be convicted then their 'sincere' remorse can count in their favour.

Non-apologies

In 1974 President Richard Nixon gave a resignation speech which included the following lines:

> I regret deeply any injuries that may have been done in the course of events that have led to this decision. I would say only that if some of my judgments were wrong, and some were wrong, they were made in what I believed at the time to be in the best interest of the nation.

Shortly after the terrorist attacks on 11 September 2001, a U.S. Republican congressman aired his views in a radio interview: 'If I saw someone that comes in [to an airport] that has a diaper on his head and a fan belt wrapped around the diaper on his head, that guy needs to be pulled over and checked.' It prompted a flood of criticism from ethnic and religious groups who regarded his comments as deeply offensive. The congressman responded:

> I regret my choice of words and in no way do I condone irrational attacks against people of Arabic ancestry, [but] the terrorists fit a profile – a terrorist profile or suspect profile. Future airport security to prevent another tragic attack on America . . . must identify those who might be terrorists.[13]

These are non-apologies, crafted to minimize personal blame and responsibility. There is the impression of an apology, but it is vague on details of the offence, the victim, the hurt caused or any remorse. Non-apologies pervade the world of politics, fashioned to manoeuvre between constituencies crucial to a public figure's standing.

A non-apology is an escape from an embarrassing or difficult situation, designed to recover authority rather than heal a hurt. Its exact phrasing is crucial, and skilled non-apologists are adept at linguistic contortion. 'Regret' is often favoured over 'sorry', since it is self-distancing. An outcome can be 'regretted' even if the act itself is not. There are words to suggest doubt about the validity of a charge, such as 'if someone was hurt', 'mistakes may have been made' and 'if some of my judgments were wrong'. The passive, conditional voice creates separation between offender and offence.

Non-apologies are fine-tuned in military parlance. The deaths of innocent civilians are often presented euphemistically and technocratically as 'collateral damage' that can 'unfortunately happen' in otherwise 'carefully targeted operations'. The pain and trauma to affected families and communities may be noted, but not dwelt upon. In 2012 the total of killed or maimed Pakistan civilians from U.S. drone strikes numbered in the thousands and reports of civilian causalities appeared regularly in the international press. In a classic non-apology, President Obama's security advisor claimed that the strikes were conducted 'in full accordance with the law' and that they 'only authorize a strike if we have a high degree of confidence that innocent civilians will not be injured or killed, except in the rarest of circumstances'. 'But', he added, despite the 'extraordinary precautions' taken, 'civilians have been accidentally injured, or worse, killed in these strikes. It is exceedingly rare, but it has happened. When it does, it pains us, and we regret it deeply, as we do any time innocents are killed in war.'[14] Note the tortuous self-validation and face-saving to minimize the problem and blame, and a half-apology to indicate that the U.S. military should not be thought of as entirely heartless.

Non-apologies are embedded in countless examples of diplomatic gamesmanship. In April 2001, for instance, there was an exchange of fire between Israeli soldiers and Palestinian security officers at a border crossing. It instantly exposed Israel to international censure at a time when its relations with the international community were strained. In a placatory gesture, the Israeli prime minister sent a letter to the U.S. Secretary of State in which he expressed 'sorrow for the regrettable incident'. The Israeli daily newspaper *Maariv* reported the event: 'The Prime Minister sent a letter to Secretary of State Colin Powell and apologized for the shooting by IDF soldiers.'[15] The switch from 'sorrow' to 'apologized' unleashed a barrage of complaints from nationalists in Israel who claimed that it undermined the status of the Israeli defence forces. A spokesperson for the prime minister rapidly issued a press release to correct that impression:

> The prime minister did not apologize and does not intend to apologize. He is simply expressing his sorrow that the incident occurred . . . The letter was written in a highly sophisticated manner. If one reads it carefully, he will notice that, in fact, the PM blames the Palestinians (for the incident) and is not apologizing for any Israeli act.[16]

The art of not saying sorry reinforces the view of politicians as Machiavellian characters, manipulating impressions to serve their own interests. There is some truth to this; nevertheless, non-apologies often suffice. They succeed in mollifying different factions sufficiently to enable the politician to carry on with more or less credibility. Careful non-apologies are the stuff of shrewd diplomacy.

In corporate public relations the non-apology is an important face-saver. A sincere apology exposes a company to compensation claims and reputational damage; the non-apology is a way out. Lloyd Blankfein was head of Goldman Sachs during the financial collapse of 2010; his non-apology stands as an archetypal illustration of the genre: 'There are . . . people who feel that we and the [banking] industry participated in things that were clearly wrong and we have reasons to regret and apologize – and some of this is real and some of this is extrapolated.'[17] Another bank non-apologizer was director of Lloyds Bank Ian Hallett. His response to the mis-selling of personal protection insurance included the following: 'We acknowledge there are cases where we could have been clearer in sales processes and as a result we didn't meet standards we set. For that we are extremely sorry if people have a cause for complaint.'[18]

A Sorry State

In February 2008 Kevin Rudd, Australian prime minister, publicly apologized for Australia's 'stolen generations' of children during the years 1869 to 1969:

> The time has now come for the nation to turn a new page in Australia's history by righting the wrongs of the past and so moving forward with confidence to the future. We apologise for the laws and policies of successive parliaments and governments that have inflicted profound grief, suffering and loss on these our fellow Australians. We apologise especially for the removal of Aboriginal and Torres Strait Islander children from their families, their communities and their country. For the pain, suffering and hurt of these stolen generations, their descendants and for their families left behind, we say sorry. To the mothers and the fathers, the brothers and the sisters, for the breaking up of families and communities, we say sorry. And for the indignity and degradation thus inflicted on a proud people and a proud culture, we say sorry.[19]

In June 2010 the British prime minister, David Cameron, apologized for the 1972 massacre of 26 unarmed civil-rights protesters and bystanders by the British Army in Northern Ireland:

> I know that some people wonder whether, nearly 40 years on from an event, [if] a prime minister needs to issue an apology. For someone of my generation, Bloody Sunday and the early 1970s are something we feel we have learnt about rather than lived through. But what happened should never,

ever have happened. The families of those who died should not have had to live with the pain and the hurt of that day and with a lifetime of loss. Some members of our armed forces acted wrongly. The government is ultimately responsible for the conduct of the armed forces and for that, on behalf of the government, indeed, on behalf of our country, I am deeply sorry.[20]

Since the mid-twentieth century there has been a remarkable growth in the number of apologies from heads of state and governments for historic wrongs. They include:

- the British role in the slave trade
- apartheid in South Africa
- the internment of Japanese Americans in the u.s.
- the seizure of Maori land in New Zealand
- Japanese war crimes in the Second World War
- the Soviet Union's massacre of Polish prisoners at the Katyn Forest in 1940
- the Vichy Government's collusion in the deportation of 320,000 French Jews to death camps
- England's unresponsiveness to the suffering of the Irish during the potato famine of the 1840s
- the 40-year Tuskegee Syphilis Study in the u.s. that deliberately withheld medical treatment for its African American subjects
- the Australian government's pressure on unwed mothers to give up their babies for adoption between the 1950s and early '70s
- the maltreatment of Brazil's Japanese community after it declared war on Japan in 1942

These apologies represent a major shift in international ethics, which have long privileged the powerful. Since the time of ancient Greece the powerful were assumed to be entitled to indulge themselves at the expense of the weak or conquered. Victims deserved their lot; after all, that is why they were victims. Apologies were neither required nor appropriate. Scholars have attributed the change to an awakening of civil and religious conscience after the Second World War.[21] Christian churches, for instance, have had to confront their role and complicity towards Jewish victims of the war, and their historic support of colonial repression in various parts of the globe. By the mid-twentieth century a swell of liberal consciousness created 'a new politics of recognition of others'. Civil rights and women's liberation movements pressed for recognition of the harms inflicted on minority groups and marginalized populations.

The profusion of state apologies has not been received un-critically. Sceptics regard them as over-inflated currency, appearing attractive but lacking substance. State apologies, they argue, hardly rank as true apologies, given that few of the apologizers were party to the original offence, and in many cases they occurred well before they were born. Why should they, and those they currently represent, bear responsibility or guilt for the sins of their predecessors? And in any case, many of those sins were not seen as sins at the time; they were an accepted part of the dominant moral order and, for the most part, legally constituted. It was so for slavery, apartheid and the Nazi racial laws of the 1930s, as abhorrent as they are to us now. What sense is there in judging a previous moral order by the standards of today and taking responsibility for it?

These are strong arguments. They surface regularly before and after state apologies. Kevin Rudd's fulsome apology to the aboriginal people came shortly after his predecessor, John Howard, adamantly refused to apologize: 'I do not believe,' explained Howard, 'as a matter of principle, that one generation can accept responsibility for the acts of an earlier generation. I don't accept that as a matter of principle.'[22]

Yet resistance to apologizing is often based less on principle and more on disputed or obfuscated facts. Turkey's unwillingness to apologize for the Armenian genocide of 1915 is a case in point: it denies there was genocide. In 1914, Turkey, then the Ottoman Empire, allied with Germany during the First World War. The Armenians in Turkey were seen as the 'enemy within' and saboteurs. Some 50 Armenian community leaders and intellectuals were arrested and executed, Armenians in the Ottoman army were disarmed and killed and Armenian property was confiscated. There were mass deportations, killings and starvation. In short, it had all the hallmarks of genocide.

But Turkey has contested this interpretation, along with the total number of deaths. Armenia claims 1.5 million people died; Turkey says it was closer to 300,000. Academics put the count at over a million. In the trading of numbers, Turkey has not denied that atrocities occurred, but says they were a consequence of the tumult of war, not a systematic attempt to destroy the Armenian people. In 2012, Turkey's Minister for European Affairs was asked on *Al Jazeera News* whether the Turkish government would recognize the events of 1915 as genocide. He responded gnomically: 'If it is recognized as a reality approved both historically and scientifically, moreover, unanimously, then why not?' Then he added, 'Would you be able to name a nation without any dark chapters or pains in its past?'[23] More than twenty countries and the European parliament have formally recognized genocide against Armenians, but within Turkey public debate has been stifled. Armenians remain one of the world's most dispersed peoples.

Similar dynamics have been at play in Japan's response to the Second World War 'comfort women'. Testimony from surviving Japanese soldiers and ex-comfort women portrays a period of brutal sexual slavery. It involved up to 200,000 young girls forced into brothels by the Japanese military across large parts of South East Asia and China. For decades the Japanese government, backed up by some Japanese historians, had maintained that much of the recruitment was voluntary and involved local prostitutes. Then, 48 years after the end of the war, the Japanese government conceded that the military had in fact been at fault. An apology was issued by Chief Cabinet Secretary Yohei Kono:

> Undeniably, this was an act, with the involvement of the military authorities of the day, that severely injured the honor and dignity of many women. The Government of Japan would like to take this opportunity once again to extend its sincere apologies and remorse to all those, irrespective of place of origin, who suffered immeasurable pain and incurable physical and psychological wounds as comfort women.[24]

This fulsome statement lacked one thing – compensation – so it was rejected by many of the victims. Following international pressure, Japan set up a private fund for donations and redress, but once again many victims opted out; they wanted compensation directly from the Japanese state as this would clearly signal Japan's responsibility for the wounds it had inflicted. Then, in 2013, in a bid to court popularity among Japan's nationalists, its prime minister questioned the Kono apology, evoking an image of Japan's past military glories. He claimed that there was no documentary evidence that comfort women were coerced and urged a revision of Kono's statement, reopening old wounds for the few remaining survivors.

Reparations and the Weight of State Apologies

Apologies can bring recognition for past wrongs, but for some people meaningful closure is impossible without reparations from those they justifiably blame, a material transaction that says amends have been made. Reparations are often vital to those who have lost loved ones or been dispossessed of their lands, property or livelihoods. Yet reparations are easier in theory than in practice. Saying sorry is cheap; reparations can be expensive and mired in legal dispute, cultural prejudice and institutional inertia. In Canada it took fourteen years of negotiations and lawsuits before the government agreed to compensate survivors of Indian Residential Schools; as children they were boarded in the schools to comply with an 1870s policy of forced assimilation. In the u.s. dispossessed Native Americans and African American farmers received a state settlement in 2012, the culmination of over 100 years of litigation. The survivors of Australia's 'stolen' aboriginal children, forcibly removed from their homes, have been less fortunate: they still await reparations. And some two decades after Rwanda's genocide, with up to a million deaths and many thousands of survivors, no government compensation has been forthcoming, despite a ruling by the Rwandan court that millions of dollars of compensation are due from the state.

Successive German leaders have expressed repentance for Germany's role in the Holocaust and Germany has paid reparations to Jewish Holocaust survivors and the State of Israel. Yet some survivors have been conspicuously absent from the reparation deal, particularly Roma and homosexuals. Like the Jews, the Roma were considered as racially inferior by the Nazis, to be rounded up and sent to concentration camps. Estimates of the number murdered vary between 220,000 and 500,000. It was not until 1979 that the West German Federal Parliament formally recognized Roma claims for compensation for their suffering, but by then most eligible claimants had died. Homosexuals were of 'special interest' to the Gestapo as early as 1934. Thousands were interned and many were among the most abused, including medical experiments to find a 'cure' for homosexuality. Legal efforts to achieve financial compensation for homosexual victims have failed, although the gay community received an official apology from the German government in 2002.

'I inherit from the past of my family, my city, my tribe, my nation a variety of debts, inheritances, rightful expectations and obligations . . . I find myself part of a history and . . . one of the bearers of a tradition.'[25] Here philosopher Alasdair MacIntyre argues for intergenerational responsibility – the moral responsibility of a state to put right the injustices it inherits from previous administrations, as well as to care for the institutions entrusted to it. Through the lens of intergenerationality the present is always tethered to the past; those who carry the responsibilities of the state also shoulder the material and emotional consequences of their predecessors' actions. They are not personally blameworthy, but as national leaders or a nation's representatives they are custodians of the legacy of blame. A state cannot create a socially responsible future without confronting its socially irresponsible past; apologies and reparations are an important, if imperfect, way forward.

8

From Blame to Restoration

Wiremu was a fifteen-year-old Maori in New Zealand. He was a worry to his teachers, parents, wider family and local community because of his antisocial attitude. Things escalated when, unlicensed, he took his mother's car for a joyride and ended up demolishing a neighbour's fence, plants and garden ornaments. He severely damaged the car. His reaction to all this was dismissive and flippant; he was much amused by what he had done.

Wiremu's actions merited police involvement and punishment, but that was not how it was handled. A *hui whakatiaka* ('putting things right meeting') with him was arranged which, following Maori custom, involved all those with whom he was closely linked. They would encourage him to take responsibility for what he had done and make amends. The meeting was non-accusatory and heartfelt. Everyone took the opportunity to praise Wiremu's strengths and achievements and how he fitted into their lives. Wiremu's mother spoke about her car; how hard it was to afford but how important it was in keeping things together: 'not much of a car, but it's mine and I'm proud of it'. There was a quiet declaration from an elderly man – it was his garden that had been damaged. He had nurtured it with his late wife whom he missed very much, and the ornaments were special gifts from her each Christmas. What happened next surprised everybody:

Wiremu stood up to speak. He was crying. He turned to the elderly neighbour whose garden he had wrecked and asked to be forgiven. He offered to help mend the fence, to sort out the plants in the garden and to repair the garden gnomes . . . Wiremu hugged his mother and apologized over and over again.[1]

Few were dry-eyed when they left the meeting. Wiremu honoured his pledges and his school conduct improved considerably.

The efficacy of indigenous restorative justice has inspired reformers of the criminal justice system. Blame-and-retribution systems of justice have several major drawbacks: they cannot guarantee that those judged guilty will feel guilty; they have a poor record in preventing reoffending; and they tend to leave victims' needs unmet. Restorative justice is an alternative. In restorative justice the offender is still blameworthy, but retribution is not the main aim. It avoids deliberately shaming or stigmatizing the offender so they are less likely to feel defensive, and it encourages involvement by all those affected by the offence.

Around 100 countries have applied a restorative justice to their criminal justice system, and restorative justice has become professionalized through a range of organizations, such as the International Institute for Restorative Practices, the Restorative Justice Council and the Center for Restorative Justice and Peacemaking. There is as yet no single term for restorative meetings between offender and offended – they have been labelled 'conferences', 'mediations', 'circles', 'boards' and 'panels'. However, all share a similar aim – to repair the harm caused by criminal behaviour through inclusive, cooperative means. Some take place when the police are initially involved, some follow charges before a trial and some are at the time of sentencing. Still others occur after sentencing, instead of, or in addition to, incarceration. Restorative justice for serious offences is usually postponed until the end of judicial proceedings.

A ground rule for restorative justice is that no party should be coerced. Meetings should be voluntary and led by skilled facilitators. Given that offenders can feel inhibited in the presence of an authoritarian figure such as a prison officer or police officer, trained volunteers or professionals from the community are generally favoured. Meetings often begin apprehensively, but as they progress participants begin to relate to one another and, at best, reach a mutual understanding. A glimpse at what takes place can be seen in an excerpt from a conference at a UK prison.[2] Sam was serving a prison sentence for burgling several homes and the conference brought him face to face with six of his victims. All were seated in a semi-circle, flanked by two facilitators. A facilitator asked Sam to explain what happened when he burgled the home of Sue and Peter:

> *Sam*: It was mid-morning. I came into town . . . I can visualize your house . . . I entered from the back, put my head round the sitting room door, went upstairs into the master bedroom. It wasn't something I felt comfortable doing. It was something that really fazed me – going into someone's sanctuary. I took some coins, membership cards and a locket. That locket destroyed me.

> *Sue (visibly upset)*: We'd gone to a funeral. I got back and could immediately see something had happened . . . It's a fear now for us, coming home . . . could he come back? I was in the lounge on my own and I felt not safe in my own home. I have to lie with my seven-year-old daughter to make her go to sleep every night. She's frightened. For us it's not property. It's the emotional impact, thinking someone's been in my bedroom. It's such an invasion – horrible thought.

> *Sam*: This situation . . . I've had so many names . . . if you're wanted . . . in prison you lose liberty . . . I had liberty but no name . . . I'm sorry I impacted on your lives. I'm sorry it's something that's still with you. I'm cursed with a memory that remembers detail. What you've said has had a big impact on me. I kidded myself I was free and easy and a decent

person. . . . I made a total mess of my life and messed up other people's lives.

Each victim heard Sam's account of burgling their home and how he now felt about it. They were generally convinced by his remorse and impressed with his plans to stop offending. Relief was palpable by the end of proceedings and there was a shared willingness to forgive Sam. In the words of one of his victims:

> You are very brave and genuine. You've got a lot to offer. You can't move on if you keep beating yourself up. I forgive you. You should make something of your life. Guilt is a horrendous thing. You've said sorry, now move ahead. You're clearly a clever bloke. Lots of prisoners would have shied away.

Not all restorative conferences are as fluent as this one. One Midwestern programme in the u.s. required juvenile offenders to write a letter of apology to their victims and read them out at their conference. It was a challenging task, many unfamiliar with letter writing and reading out loud. It came over as stilted, as noted by some of the victims:

> Well, to be honest with you, I think that everyone else thought that he was . . . like, 'Hey, I'm here. I'm reading this letter that I was told to write.'

• • •

> Dan did read some flaky letter that he wrote. I shouldn't say flaky, but it wasn't very heartfelt. It didn't come off sounding really truthful.[3]

Despite these difficulties, restorative criminal justice has a positive record. The evidence shows that, compared to traditional justice, offenders commit fewer repeat crimes and their victims' desire for revenge and blame is much reduced. It helps them recover from their psychological injuries, including post-traumatic stress.[4] The costs of restorative justice, its advocates claim, are amply offset by the savings on court appearances that fail to bring offenders to justice, and the reduced use of costly incarceration.

Restorative Justice in Schools

Confronted with large classes and rule-resistant students, many schools have instituted zero tolerance policies for serious infringements, such as carrying weapons, sexual assault or distributing drugs. They typically bring immediate suspension or exclusion. Zero tolerance has also been extended to much lesser infractions – non-violent misbehaviour, the wrong dress code, eating in class or lateness.[5] In one U.S. kindergarten children were sent home for bringing paper clips, toy guns or cough drops into school.[6] The toughness of the response, in the eyes of its supporters, is its major strength – it puts blame where blame is due with uncompromising consequences for rule breakers.

Yet barring a student from school has been shown to discriminate against minorities, leaving a trail of resentment and stigma that disrupts the student's education and progress. Moreover, suspending or excluding a student for violence or drug use often fails to tackle the behaviour, but pushes the student further along the school-to-prison pipeline.[7] These issues have steered some educational authorities towards restorative justice.[8]

The San Francisco Board of Education, for example, embarked on a restorative justice project in 2009. Students who would normally be ejected for stealing, talking back or fighting, were instead asked to work out solutions with the help of teachers and parents. They were encouraged to talk things through before matters got out of hand, to listen to each other and to apologize. After three years the results were assessed. Across the district expulsions had fallen by an average of 44 per cent and suspensions by 35 per cent. Punishment became a last, not first, resort, a major cultural shift for staff and students alike:

> *School principal*: In the past, we defaulted to the most expedient thing. Student behavior is incorrect, student gets suspended – not really fully thinking through the process and asking whether this is a good educational decision for this particular student.

> *Student*: The teacher doesn't yell or send anyone out of class. Instead we circle up and everybody gets a say in how to fix it . . . It's boring, most of the time, but it's better than everybody being angry. That's how it is in my house.[9]

In 2004 a UK study tracked 625 restorative justice conferences across nine different schools. Common reasons for calling a conference were bullying, assault, violent behaviour, name-calling, verbal abuse, family feuds, fractured relationships, theft and malicious gossip. The investigators found that the vast majority of conferences produced successful agreements – only 4 per cent were broken after three months. Many initially sceptical parents were won over and most teachers were pleased with the outcomes:

> *Head teacher*: Two of our boys vandalised a primary school last week. Conferences were used to bring the boys face-to-face with staff from the school, during which apologies were made and reparation agreed. This is very powerful.[10]

The majority of students thought that the conferences were fair and helped them to defuse their simmering anger or rancour:

> We all told the truth. I think it was because we were all in the room together and listening to what everybody was saying.

It made it harder not to tell the truth. I'm glad I didn't tell fibs because it was all sorted out in the end.

• • •

We both had the chance to tell our side of things without being interrupted. It made a change for adults to listen to us. I felt respected, as a person, rather than being treated as a child and told what to do.

The outcomes of school restorative justice have been encouraging. It has not meant a wholesale abandonment of zero tolerance: some schools will draw the line at sexual assault or serious physical injury. Others, however, have been intent on keeping students away from the criminal justice system as long as possible, regardless of offence.[11]

A school principal who is serious about restorative justice is likely to be embarking on a cultural change that challenges some long-standing assumptions about school discipline, in particular the idea that the teacher is firmly in charge and is there to dispense justice. The shift away from this requires careful staff support and training. In addition, as restorative conferences can be time-consuming to arrange and supervise, they may not fit easily into a tightly packed teaching schedule. Some restructuring and resourcing may be necessary to ease the pathway.

In the Workplace

Workplace restorative justice has received less attention than restorative justice in schools and the criminal justice system, but has been recommended for tackling blame wars, harassment, bullying and discrimination at work.[12] A restorative consultant describes how it helped resolve a case of interpersonal conflict:

Two individuals, Jane and Richard, were working at the headquarters of a large organization . . . Over a period of time a number of small incidents and disagreement led to a breakdown in communications . . . They openly criticized each other's work in front of colleagues . . . Things came to a head when they began to argue with each other at a public meeting attended by the head of the organization. This was reported back to the manager and it was decided to offer them the opportunity to discuss the issues in a restorative conference . . . The restorative conference that followed allowed both parties to have their say, listen to each other, and realize the harm they were causing each other and to the organization itself. As a result of this meeting both parties undertook to cease such damaging behaviour, and personal development plans were put in place to address their respective shortcomings, together with a review at stages to ensure compliance and progress.[13]

Some people at work are more at ease than others with restorative processes. Simon Green and colleagues at the University of Hull were keen to find out why. They evaluated the operation of a major programme designed to bring restorative conferencing to a wide range of community work teams in a UK city, part of a plan to make the city more restorative in style.[14] They found that people who held client-facing jobs were already familiar with dealing with feelings, so they soon adapted to restorative meetings. As their confidence grew, restoration was adopted for problems such as lateness, absence, workloads and contracts, reducing the recourse to formal grievance procedures.

It enables you to talk about difficult situations in an open manner and if you've been listened to and had the chance to discuss and you have heard then you have accept to agree to disagree.[15]

• • •

It changed the way we work because now we can spend more time with people and get down to the real reasons behind why they have done something.[16]

But staff groups with little prior experience or training in communication skills were perplexed by restorativeness, often dismissing it as 'another management fad'. They struggled with their unfamiliar role in conferences:

Manager: Many people don't have the ability to explain themselves and fly into anger and insults because they cannot vocalize their true meaning. If they feel like they are losing an argument they will get up and walk out because they have not learned to do things any other way.[17]

In sum, workplace restoration is more than a set of techniques. It is a way of thinking and feeling about human relationships and conflict resolution, but alien to those conditioned to defending their corner when blamed. Indeed, and ironically, while restorative justice has grown in the criminal justice system, police officers have struggled to apply it to themselves when they receive complaints about their service.[18] Restoration is discomforting for many police officers: they feel vulnerable and a loss of control. The outcomes of conferences have often been tokenistic and there is reluctance to apologize to a complainant. Nevertheless, official reviews have recommended that face-to-face, independent mediation and restorative methods should, wherever possible, replace internal, police-managed complaints systems – a cultural shift aimed at improving public trust.[19]

Truth and (Some) Reconciliation

The boldest form of restorative justice is the truth and reconciliation commission. It confronts the anguish, endemic blame and pain that rip communities apart after civil wars and human rights abuses. Commissions attempt to heal the deepest wounds and help a community move forward. They offer perpetrators and their victims a platform from which they can express their candid feelings about the harm suffered and done and, if possible, achieve some reconciliation and peace. Proceedings are typically steered by a high-ranking figure, someone who bears witness to perpetrators' crimes and who can in some instances recommend an amnesty.

There have been truth and reconciliation commissions in Sierra Leone, Peru, Guatemala, Morocco, Liberia and the Solomon Islands, but all are overshadowed by South Africa's, formed in 1996. It aimed to lance the wounds of apartheid and help the country move towards an all-inclusive democracy. The chairperson was Archbishop Desmond Tutu, a man of considerable moral authority in the Christian community and beyond. His theological perspective shaped proceedings: that victims may rise above their hurt and wounds and bear the pain of forgiving those who confess their crimes, and that repentance and forgiveness would enrich the wider community and create a deeper way of living with others.

The South African commission has been judged a qualified success.[20] There were some remarkable confessions, such as Eugene de Kock's. De Kock ran the South African government's notorious hit squad, Vlakplaas, his meticulous work earning him the nickname of 'Prime Evil'. After killing his target he would incinerate or blow up the remains so that all evidence was destroyed. His 'one-armed bandits', as he called them, were student activists whom he rigged with grenades that exploded, leaving them dead or maimed. De Kock expressed remorse for what he had done:

> We wasted the most precious gift, which is life . . . I would like to tell those families that I am very sorry about it . . . There are times when I wish I wasn't born. I can't tell you how dirty I feel. I shouldn't have joined the South African

Police. We achieved nothing. We just left hatred behind us. There are children who will never know their parents and I will have to carry this burden for ever. I'm a very private person and I don't like to show emotion, but I sympathise with my victims as if they were my own children. This is all I can say.[21]

His declaration was applauded by a black audience and the South African press described it as an extraordinary turn-around. Victims and their relatives praised his admissions and some said that their long hatred of him was now beginning to fade. But not everyone was persuaded; their revulsion was too entrenched. One observer described his arrogance up until the moment he was convicted: 'On that day De Kock changed his whole strategy. He became a man obsessed with remorse.'[22]

It takes considerable courage to face a past tormentor. Thandi Shezi's friends understood this, but persuaded her to take part in the South African commission because they felt it might release her from her demons. She had long been silent about her terrible ordeal at the hands of the South African police: they had arrested her for membership of an anti-apartheid activist group, repeatedly beaten, raped and electrocuted her, and held her in solitary confinement for a year. She faced her oppressor in trepidation, but expected him to acknowledge what he had done and then she would be prepared to forgive him. But the outcome was very different: he denied all knowledge of her. 'You are the one who suggested a black policeman should put a sack over my head', she cried in frustration. 'You are the one.' He replied that he could not remember her.[23]

Forgiveness is pivotal to restorative justice and is celebrated among major religions. Forgiveness means relinquishing the urge to blame, and pardoning one's tormenter. Research indicates that, following remorse or a plea for compassion, forgiving can be psychologically liberating for victims, improving their confidence, happiness and health.[24]

Yet sometimes it is impossible to forgive. Psychologists point to the emotional costs of this – the stress of unresolved anger and blame. Less commonly mentioned are the exceptions to this rule – it is not always destructive. Psychotherapist Jeanne Safer points to 'moral unforgivers' who hold on to their outrage and hurt, but then turn it outwards to fight against a recurrence of the crimes that have been committed against them and others.[25] To not forgive is an unequivocal sign that the culpability of some perpetrators should never be compromised. It says that there are moral lines that should never be crossed, and there should be no peace for those who deny others their very humanity. Elie Wiesel, survivor of Nazi concentration camps, is blunt in his non-forgiveness: 'I hope that I will never forgive the murderers. I do not want God to forgive them for the things they did to the children. Never.'[26]

A Final Thought:
The Trouble With Blame

A man can get discouraged many times but he is not a failure until he begins to blame somebody else and stops trying.

John Burroughs, American naturalist

It is tempting to end a book on blame with a vision of a world where blame plays no part. It would be an engaging fantasy, but would miss the point: blame is not always a bad thing. It can begin to right wrong or injustice; it can ring alarm bells about lines that should not be crossed; it can hold the powerful – a corporation, a government, an abuser – to account. Blame is a moral manager and without it the very essence of law and of being a law-abiding citizen is undercut. If we cannot blame or be blamed then legality has no cultural purchase. Blame will not, and should not, go away.

The trouble with blame is not blame per se, but how it is twisted and abused. Ego protection often trumps empathy in the blame game: pride, possessiveness and self-aggrandisement are enduring human drives. Blame can be exploited as a political tool to gain ascendancy or power; it can be harnessed to denigrate a national, racial, gender, religious or ethnic group; it can be inflated to score accusatory points. Emotionally charged, blame is capable of destroying marriages, terminating friendships and dividing nations. It is a remarkable resource for ill intent.

It is very easy to resort to the language of blame – too easy. Blaming a person or a people simplifies matters; it bypasses the complexity of circumstances that lead to an outcome. However, when blame is spread liberally across our daily affairs it loses its discriminatory power; it thrusts liability onto others and creates defensiveness, exonerating ourselves and closing down opportunities for change or transformation. When everyone blames everyone else options are limited, beyond continued rancour or conflict.

None of this will disappear, but we are not entirely victims of our urges, nor are we helpless at creating better structures to contain and channel blame – some thoughts on these matters appear in the preceding pages. A linguistic shift could help: how we talk affects how we work and how others react. Conversations about 'difficulties', 'mutual responsibilities' and 'problem sharing' are likely to escape some of the emotional and accusative baggage we attach to blame, especially the perniciousness of scapegoating. It behoves leaders, teachers and trainers to encourage others to see situations from more than one perspective, to stand back before judging their fellow citizens. The smart move is to opt out of the blame game altogether and certainly be wary about panicky press reports that demonize.

Many institutions, wittingly or unwittingly, trade on blame, but blame cultures and unethical practices are not inevitable. They are produced within regimes of anxiety and fear, where surveillance is obsessive and finger-pointing the method of control. All this can be shifted with leadership that treats whistle-blowers as organizational assets, not pariahs, that puts restoration above recrimination, and that promotes trust and collaboration.

Finally, we are not powerless to repair some of the damage and injuries of blame. The gradual spread of restorative justice is cause for optimism, and knowing when and how to apologize, even for historical grievances, can soothe sores and begin a process of healing.

References

1 Why Do We Blame?

1 Human Rights Council, Twelfth session, Agenda item 4, 'Human Rights Situations that Require the Council's Attention' (7 September 2009), p. 2.

2 Sujeet Kumar, 'Gang Blinds Indian Woman, Accused of Witchcraft, with Scissors', Reuters (21 May 2011).

3 Mark Oppenheimer, 'On a Visit to the u.s., A Nigerian Witch-hunter Explains Herself', *New York Times* (21 May 2010).

4 'Witchcraft-based Child Abuse: Action Plan Launched', bbc News (14 August 2012); Antonia Simon, Hanan Hauari, Katie Hollingworth, and John Vorhaus, 'A Rapid Literature Review of Evidence on Child Abuse Linked to Faith or Belief', cwrc Working Paper, 15 (2012).

5 James G. Frazer, *The Golden Bough: A Study in Magic and Religion* (London, 1920), vol. 12, Part 15.

6 According to the sixth-century-bc poet Hipponax.

7 Betty M. Adelson, *The Lives of Dwarfs: Their Journey from Public Curiosity Toward Social Liberation* (New Brunswick, nj, 2005), p. 10.

8 'I am the Office Scapegoat: I Loathe Going to Work . . .', www.officepolitics.com, accessed 1 March 2014.

9 'Bullying at Work', European Agency for Safety and Health at Work Fact Sheet 23, 2002; 'Results of the 2010 wbi u.s. Workplace Bullying Survey', www.workplacebullying.org, accessed 23 May 2014.

10 Kurt Schimmel and Jeananne Nicholls, 'Workplace Cyber Bullying: A Research Agenda', in *Bullying in the Workplace:*

Symptoms, Causes and Remedies, ed. J. Lipinski and L. M. Crothers (London, 2013), pp. 223–34.

11 Heather McLaughlin, Christopher Uggen and Amy Blackstone, 'Sexual Harassment, Workplace Authority, and the Paradox of Power', *American Sociological Review*, LXXVII/4 (2012), pp. 625–47.

12 Carl G. Jung, *The Archetypes and the Collective Unconscious* (London, 1968).

13 Dorothy Haller, 'Bastardy and Baby Farming in Victorian England', *Student Historical Journal* (Loyola University), 21 (1990), n.p, at www.loyno.edu.

14 See Leontine R. Young, 'Personality Patterns in Unmarried Mothers', in *The Unwed Mother*, ed. R. W. Roberts (York, 1996), pp. 81–94. John Bolby, director of the prestigious Tavistock Clinic in London, regarded an illegitimate baby as a symptom of the mother's neurosis, concluding that the mothers were psychopathic and defective.

15 Extracts taken from 'Senate Inquiry into Forced Adoptions Releases Report', www.aph.gov.au, accessed 13 April 2013.

16 Alison Park, J. Curtice, K. Thomson, M. Phillips, E. Clery and S. Butt, eds, *British Social Attitudes: The 26th Report* (London, 2010).

17 See Rich Morin, 'The Public Renders a Split Verdict on Changes in Family Structure', Pew Research Social and Demographic Trends (Washington, 2011); Pat Thane and Tanay Evans, *Sinners? Scroungers? Saints? Unmarried Motherhood in Twentieth-century England* (Oxford, 2012).

18 E. Kouichi, 'Shirayanagi Spokeswoman Souad Abderrahim: Single Mothers are a Disgrace to Tunisia', www.tunisia-live.net, 9 November 2011.

19 Shveta Kalyanwala, Francis Zavier, Shireen Jejeebhoy and Kumar Rajesh, 'Abortion Experiences of Unmarried Young Women in India: Evidence from a Facility-based Study in Bihar and Jharkhand', *International Perspectives on Sexual and Reproductive Health*, XXXVI/2 (2010), pp. 62–71.

20 Fritz Heider, *The Psychology of Interpersonal Relations* (London, 2013); Kelly G. Shaver, *The Attribution of Blame: Causality, Responsibility, and Blameworthiness* (New York, 1985).

21 See Roy Baumeister and Kathleen Vohs, 'Four Roots of Evil', in *The Social Psychology of Good and Evil*, ed. Arthur. G. Miller (New York, 2004), pp. 85–101; Roy Baumeister, *Evil: Inside Human Violence and Cruelty* (Oxford, 1999).

22 Amy Grubb and Julie Harrower, 'Understanding Attribution of Blame in Cases of Rape: An Analysis of Participant Gender, Type of Rape and Perceived Similarity to the Victim', *Journal of Sexual Aggression*, xv/1 (2009), pp. 63–81.

23 Charles Darwin, *The Descent of Man* (New York, 1871), p. 157.

24 Barbara Kellerman, 'Leadership Warts and All', *Harvard Business Review*, lxxxii/1 (2004), pp. 40–45; Daniel R. Schwarz, *Endtimes? Crises and Turmoil at the New York Times* (New York, 2012).

25 Ransdell Pierson, *The Queen of Mean: The Unauthorized Biography of Leona Helmsley* (New York, 1989); Ronald H. Jensen, 'Reflections on United States v. Leona Helmsley: Should "Impossibility" be a Defense to Attempted Income Tax Evasion?', *Virginia Tax Review*, xii/335 (1992), pp. 335–96. See also 'Leona Helmsley Biography', www.biography.com, accessed 9 April 2014.

26 Keith Wagstaff, 'Why So Many Russians Still Love Stalin', *The Week* (5 March 2013).

27 Annabel Venning, 'How Picasso Who Called All Women Goddesses or Doormats Drove his Lovers to Despair and Even Suicide with his Cruelty and Betrayal', *MailOnline* (7 March 2012).

28 Martin Niemöller, 'First They Came'. The exact provenance of the elegy is uncertain but Professor Harold Marcuse of the University of California concludes that the piece most likely emerged in 1946 and definitely took on the well-known poetic form by the early 1950s. See 'Martin Niemöller's Famous Quotation', www.history.ucsb.edu, 28 February 2013.

29 Victoria Barnett, *Bystanders: Conscience and Complicity during the Holocaust* (Westport, CT, 1999).

30 Gene Currivan, 'Nazi Death Factory Shocks Germans on a Forced Tour, *New York Times* (18 April 1945), pp.1, 8.

31 Tiziana Pozzoli and Gianluca Gini, 'Why do Bystanders of Bullying Help or Not? A Multidimensional Model', *Journal of Early Adolescence*, XXXIII/3 (2013), pp. 315–40.

32 Maureen Scully and Mary Rowe, 'Bystander Training Within Organizations', *Journal of the International Ombudsman Association,* II/1 (2009), pp. 1–9; Karen Mitchell and Jennifer Freitag, 'Forum Theatre for Bystanders: A New Model for Gender Violence Prevention', *Violence Against Women*, XVII/8 (2011), pp. 990–1013.

33 Dacher Keltner and Jason Marsh, 'We Are All Bystanders', *Greater Good* (1 September 2006).

34 Max Hastings, 'Years of Liberal Dogma Have Spawned a Generation of Amoral, Uneducated, Welfare Dependent, Brutalised Youngsters', *Daily Mail* (10 August 2011).

35 Samuel Johnson, *A Journey to the Western Islands of Scotland* (Dublin, 1775), chapter 2, p. 7.

36 Frank H. Stewart, *Honor* (Chicago, 1994).

37 Patricia Mosquera, Anthony Manstead and Agneta Fischer, 'Honor in the Mediterranean and Northern Europe, *Journal of Cross-cultural Psychology*, XXXIII/1 (2002), pp.16–36.

38 Stephen Wilson, *Feuding, Conflict, and Banditry in Nineteenth-century Corsica* (Cambridge, 2003).

39 United Nations Population Fund, 'Ending Violence against Women and Girls', in *State of the World Population* (New York, 2000), chapter 3.

40 James Bowman, *Honor: A History* (New York, 2007), pp. 5–6.

41 Christian Smith, Kari Christoffersen, Hilary Davidson and Patricia Herzog, *Lost in Transition: The Dark Side of Emerging Adulthood* (Oxford, 2011), p. 28.

2 Panics Old and New

1 Stanley Cohen, *Folk Devils and Moral Panics: The Creation of the Mods and the Rockers* (Oxford, 1972), p. 29.

2 Robert Hughes, *The Fatal Shore* (London, 2003), p. 27.

3 Trevor Cullen, 'HIV/AIDS: 20 Years of Press Coverage', *Australian Studies in Journalism*, XXII (2003), pp. 63–82.

4 Jenny Kitzinger, 'A Sociology of Media Power: Key Issues in Audience Reception Research', in *Message Received*, ed. G. Philo (Harlow, 1999).

5 Klaus Neumann and Gwenda Tavan, *Does History Matter? Making and Debating Citizenship, Immigration and Refugee Policy in Australia and New Zealand* (Canberra, 2009).

6 Ceri Mollard, *Asylum: The Truth Behind The Headlines* (Oxford, 2001).

7 Kerry Moore, Paul Mason and Justin Lewis, *Images of Islam in the UK: The Representation of British Muslims in the National Print News Media, 2000–2008* (Cardiff, 2008).

8 Melanie Phillips, *Londonistan* (New York, 2007).

9 'Muslim-Western Tensions Persist', *Pew Global Attitudes Project* (Washington, DC, 2011); Henri Nickels, Lyn Thomas, Mary Hickman and Sara Silvestri, 'Constructing "Suspect" Communities and Britishness: Mapping British Press Coverage of Irish and Muslim Communities, 1974–2007', *European Journal of Communication*, XXVII/2 (2012), pp. 135–51.

10 Christopher Bail, 'The Fringe Effect Civil Society Organizations and the Evolution of Media Discourse about Islam Since the September 11th Attacks', *American Sociological Review*, LXXVII/6 (2012), pp. 855–79, 69.

11 Nahid Kabir, 'Representation of Islam and Muslims in the Australian Media', *Journal of Muslim Minority Affairs*, XXVI/3 (2006), pp. 313–28.

12 Abu Dhabi Gallup, 'Muslim Americans: Faith, Freedom, and the Future', www. gallup.com, August 2011.

13 David Miller, 'Propaganda and the "Terror Threat" in the UK', in *Muslims and the News Media*, ed. E. Poole and J. Richardson (London, 2006).

14 *Daily Mirror* (18 July 2000).

15 See web video by Robert Booth, Guy Grandjean and Noah Payne-Frank, 'Vigilante Paedophile Hunters Dispense Morally Dubious Justice', www.theguardian.com, 25 October 2013.

16 Personal communication.

17 Glenn Wilson and David Cox, *The Child-lovers: A Study of Paedophiles in Society* (London, 1983).

18 Kieran McCartan, 'Current Understandings of Paedophilia and the Resulting Crisis in Modern Society', in *Psychological Sexual Dysfunctions*, ed. J. Caroll and M. Alena (New York, 2008), pp. 51–84.

19 Alex Hossack, Sally Playle, Abie Spencer and Anna Carey, 'Helpline: Accessible Help Inviting Active or Potential Paedophiles', *Journal of Sexual Aggression*, X/1 (2004), pp. 123–32.

3 Blame Cultures

1 James Reason, *The Human Contribution: Unsafe Acts, Accidents and Heroic Recoveries* (Farnham, 2008).

2 Sidney Dekker, *Just Culture: Balancing Safety and Accountability* (Farnham, 2012).

3 Chris Argyris, 'Double-loop Learning in Organizations, *Harvard Business Review*, LV/5 (1977), pp. 115–25.

4 International Civil Aviation Organization Working Paper, 'High-level Safety Conference' (Montreal, 2010).

5 Allan Frankel, Michael Leonard and Charles Denham, 'Fair and Just Culture, Team Behavior, and Leadership Engagement: The Tools to Achieve High Reliability', *Health Services Research*, XLI (2006), pp. 1690–709; Jill Setaro and Mary Connolly, 'Safety Huddles in the PACU: When a Patient Self-medicates', *Journal of PeriAnesthesia Nursing*, XXVI/2 (2011), pp. 96–102.

6 Louise Hunt, 'Case Review Model Aims to End Social Work Blame Culture', *Community Care* (27 March 2012).

7 Health and Safety Executive, '£55,000 For Teacher Who Slipped on a Chip', www.hse.gov.uk, accessed 19 April 2014.

8 Helen Carter, 'Teacher Wins £14,000 for Fall from Toilet', *The Guardian* (23 April 2007).

9 Liebeck v. McDonald's Restaurants, New Mexico District Court, 18 August 1994.

10 CNNMoney, 'McDonald's Obesity Suit Tossed', www.money.cnn.com, 17 February 2003.

11 Andrew Hough, 'Lauren Rosenberg: US Woman Sues Google after Maps Directions Caused Accident', *The Telegraph* (2 June 2010).

12 Polly Rippon, 'Sheffield Fake Bus Injury Claims', *The Star* (18 August 2013).

13 'Beware Falling Acorns! Health and Safety Lunacy Reaches New Peak with Warning Sign', *Daily Mail* (14 October 2010).

14 Kathleen Kendall and Rose Wiles, 'Resisting Blame and Managing Emotion in General Practice: The Case of Patient Suicide', *Social Science and Medicine*, LXX/11 (2010), p. 1716.

15 Natasha Deonarain, 'I Was Sued and Lived to Tell the Tale', www.kevinmd.com, 17 January 2013.

16 Osman Ortashi, Jaspal Virdee, Rudaina Hassan, Tomasz Mutrynowski and Fikri Abu-Zidan, 'The Practice of Defensive Medicine Among Hospital Doctors in the United Kingdom', *BMC Medical Ethics*, XIV/1 (2013), p. 42.

17 Manish Sethi, William Obremskey, Hazel Natividad, Hassan Mir and Alex Jahangir, 'Incidence and Costs of Defensive Medicine Among Orthopedic Surgeons in the United States: A National Survey Study', *American Journal of Orthopedics* (February 2012), pp. 69–73.

18 'Doctors and Other Health Professionals Report Fear of Malpractice Has a Big, and Mostly Negative, Impact on Medical Practice, Unnecessary Defensive Medicine and Openness in Discussing Medical Errors', www.thefreelibrary.com, 7 February 2003.

19 Michelle Mello, Amitabh Chandra, Atul Gawande and David Studdert, 'National Costs of the Medical Liability System', *Health Affairs*, xxix/9 (2010), pp. 1569–77.

20 Michael Power, 'Evaluating the Audit Explosion', *Law and Policy*, xxv/3 (2003), pp. 199–200.

21 Carina Furåker, 'Nurses' Everyday Activities in Hospital Care', *Journal of Nursing Management*, xvii/3 (2009), p. 270.

22 Beda Sweeney, 'Audit Team Defence Mechanisms: Auditee Influence', *Accounting and Business Research*, xli/4 (2011), pp. 333–56.

23 Irvine Lapsley, 'New Public Management: The Cruellest Invention of the Human Spirit?', *Abacus*, xlv/1 (2009), p. 13.

24 Simon Reed, 'Restoring Discretion', Annual Conference of the Confederation of Police Officers in England and Wales, Blackpool, 15 May 2007.

4 Blaming the Organization

1 For example, '10 Most-hated Companies in America', *Wall Street Journal* (14 January 2013).

2 'In Your Community: McDonald's Educational Resource Materials', www.mcdonaldseducates.com, accessed 22 April 2014.

3 Joel Bakan, *The Corporation: The Pathological Pursuit of Profit and Power* (New York, 2005).

4 Ingrid Eckerman, 'Chemical Industry and Public Health: Bhopal as an Example', www.ima.kth.se, 2001.

5 Roli Varma and Daya Varma, 'The Bhopal Disaster of 1984', *Bulletin of Science, Technology and Society*, xxv/1 (2005), pp. 37–45.

6 Edward Broughton, 'The Bhopal Disaster and its Aftermath: A Review', *Environmental Health*, iv/6 (2005), pp. 1–6.

7 Ingrid Eckerman, *The Bhopal Saga: Causes and Consequences of the World's Largest Industrial Disaster* (India, 2005).

8 Lydia Polgreen and Haro Kumar, '8 Former Executives Guilty in '84 Bhopal Chemical Lead', *New York Times* (7 June 2010); 'Lack of Evidence Held up Anderson Extradition: MEA', *Times of India*, www.timesofindia.indiatimes.com,10 June 2010.

9 Aaron Duff, 'Punitive Damages in Maritime Torts: Examining Shipowners' Punitive Damage Liability in the Wake of the Exxon Valdez Decision', *Seton Hall Law Review*, XXXIX/3(2011), pp. 955–79.

10 Mark Thiessen, 'Court Orders $507.5 Million Damages in Exxon Valdez Spill', *Huffington Post* (15 May 2009).

11 Sean Cockerham, '25 Years Later, Oil Spilled from Exxon Valdez Still Clings to Lives, Alaska Habitat', *Anchorage Daily News* (21 March 2014); Joanna Walters, 'Exxon Valdez: 25 Years After the Alaska Oil Spill, the Court Battle Continues', *The Telegraph* (23 March 2014); Kirsten Stade, 'Exxon Valdez Recovery Remains Stuck In Limbo', www.peer.org, 15 July 2013.

12 Sucheta Dalal, 'Death of a Whistleblower: The Satyendra Dubey Story', www.suchetadalal.com, 3 December 2003.

13 Marie Brenner, 'The Man Who Knew Too Much', *Vanity Fair* (May 1996).

14 National Resource Center, 'National Business Ethics Survey: How Employees View Ethics in Their Organization – 1994–2005' (Washington, DC, 2005).

15 Brita Bjørkelo, Stale Einarsen, Morten Nielsen and Stig Matthiesen, 'Silence is Golden? Characteristics and Experiences of Self-reported Whistleblowers', *European Journal of Work and Organizational Psychology*, XX/2 (2011), pp. 206–38; Jessica Mesmer-Magnus and Chockalingam Viswesvaran, 'Whistleblowing in Organizations: An Examination of Correlates of Whistleblowing Intentions, Actions, and Retaliation', *Journal of Business Ethics*, LXII/3 (2005), pp. 277–97.

16 Marcia Miceli, James Van Scotter, Janet Near and Michael Rehg, 'Responses to Perceived Organizational Wrongdoing: Do Perceiver Characteristics Matter?', in *Social Influences on Ethical Behaviour*, ed. J. M. Darley, D. M. Messick and T. R. Tyler (London, 2009), pp. 119–35.

17 Stephanos Avakian and Joanne Roberts, 'Whistleblowers in Organisations: Prophets at Work?', *Journal of Business Ethics*, cx/1 (2012), pp. 1–14.

18 Richard Lacayo and Amanda Ripley, 'Persons of the Year 2002: The Whistleblowers Sherron Watkins of Enron, Coleen Rowley of the FBI, Cynthia Cooper of WorldCom', *Time* (30 December 2002).

19 Stephen Foley, 'Enron Whistleblower Tells Court of Lay Lies', *The Independent* (16 March 2006); 'Whistleblower Recalls Enron Crisis', www.news.bbc.co.uk, 12 September 2006.

20 Cynthia Cooper, *Extraordinary Circumstances: The Journey of a Corporate Whistleblower* (New Jersey, 2009); Greg Farrel, 'WorldCom's Whistle-blower Tells Her Story', *USAToday*, www.usatoday30.usatoday.com, 14 February 2008.

21 Jennifer Bayot, 'Ebbers Sentenced to 25 Years in Prison for $11 Billion Fraud', *New York Times* (13 July 2005).

22 David Griffin, *The 9/11 Commission Report: Omissions and Distortions* (Northampton, MA, 2005); 'Coleen Rowley', www.americanswhotellthetruth.org, accessed 16 June 2014.

23 Stephen Campion, 'Whistleblowing: Managing Vexatious Complaints', The Hospital Consultants and Specialists Association (7 January 2012).

24 IRS, 'Whistleblower – Informant Award', www.irs.gov, accessed 23 April 2014.

25 'Whistleblowers Flood China's Anti-Corruption Hotline', *People's Daily Online* (30 June 2009).

26 Marleen Nicholson, 'McLibel: A Case Study in English Defamation Law', *Wisconsin International Law Journal*, xviii/1 (2000), pp. 1–145.

27 Francis Lloyd, 'McLibel: Burger Culture on Trial', *University of Queensland Law Journal*, xx/2 (1999), pp. 340–44; Matt Haig, *Brand Failures: The Truth About the 100 Biggest Branding Mistakes of all Time* (London, 2005).

28 Student/Farmworker Alliance, 'Victory over Taco Bell', www.sfalliance.org, accessed 22 April 2014.

29 Stacy Tessier, 'Rethinking the Food Chain: Farmworkers and the Taco Bell Boycott', *Journal of Developing Societies*, XXXIII/1–2 (2007), pp. 89–97; Duncan Campbell, 'Farmworkers Win Historic Deal After Boycotting Taco Bell', *The Guardian* (12 March 2005).

30 Tescopoly, 'Local Shops', www.old.tescopoly.cucumber.netuxo.co.uk, accessed 22 April 2014.

31 Owen Bowcott, 'Bristol Riot over New Tesco Store Leaves Eight Police Officers Injured', *The Guardian* (22 April 2011).

32 Patrick Kingsley, 'Stokes Croft: The Art of Protest', *The Guardian* (26 May 2011); '"Pay the Fine" Mug Sale Successful: Funds Raised', www.boycotttesco.wordpress.com, 7 May 2012.

33 John Barker, 'Carnival against Capitalism', www.vgpolitics.f9.co.uk, June 1999.

34 Barbara Ehrenreich, *Dancing in the Streets: A History of Collective Joy* (London, 2007), pp. 259–60; Benjamin Shepard, *Play, Creativity, and Social Movements: If I Can't Dance, It's Not My Revolution* (London, 2011).

35 Beautiful Trouble, 'The Teddy Bear Catapult', www.beautifultrouble, accessed 23 April 2014.

36 Adbusters, 'About Adbusters', www.adbusters.org, accessed 23 April 2014.

37 The Yes Men, 'Identity Correction', www.theyesmen.org, accessed 28 April 2014.

38 'Bhopal Disaster – BBC – The Yes Men', www.youtube.com, 2 January 2007.

39 'Bhopal Hoax Sends Dow Stock Down', www.cnn.com, 3 December 2004; Carl Bialik, 'BBC is Victim of Hoax in Report on Bhopal', *Wall Street Journal* (6 December 2004).

40 Dagny Nome, 'Culture Jamming', Copenhagen Business School unpublished paper, www.anthrobase.com, 2001.

41 Naomi Klein, *No Logo: Taking Aim at the Brand Bullies* (Toronto, 2000), p. 297.

42 See WANGO, 'NGO Handbook', www.wango.org, 18 February 2010.

43 Matthew Hilton, James McKay, Nicholas Crowson and Jean-Francois Mouhot, *The Politics of Expertise: How NGOs Shaped Modern Britain* (Oxford, 2013).

44 P. J. Simmons, 'Learning to Live With NGOs', *Foreign Policy*, CXII (Autumn 1988), p. 83.

45 Peter Willetts, *Non-governmental Organizations in World Politics: The Construction of Global Governance* (Oxford, 2010).

46 Jon Burchell and Joanne Cook, 'Banging on Open Doors? Stakeholder Dialogue and the Challenge of Business Engagement for UK NGOs', *Environmental Politics,* xx/6 (2011), p. 927.

47 Earth First!, 'About Earth First!', www.earthfirst.org, accessed 21 April 2014.

48 Ibid.

49 Tony Rice and Paula Owen, *Decommissioning the Brent Spar* (London, 2003); Ragnar Löfstedt and Ortwin Renn, 'The Brent Spar Controversy: An Example of Risk Communication Gone Wrong', *Risk Analysis*, XIII/2 (1997), pp. 131–6.

50 Kristian Tangen, 'Shell: Struggling to Build a Better World?', The Fridtjof Nansen Institute, Report 1 (2003).

51 'About Us', www.citizen.org, accessed 8 October 2014.

5 The Empires Strike Back

1 Nicky Hager and Bob Burton, *Secrets and Lies* (Nelson, New Zealand, 1999).

2 Ibid. p. 32.

3 Ibid. pp. 120–21.

4 Ibid. pp. 35, 38.

5 Ibid. pp. 159–67.

6 Ibid. pp. 35–6.

7 Ibid. p. 43.

8 Ibid. p. 72.

9 A full account of this event is reported in SourceWatch, 'When Helicopters Attack: A Near Accident Leads to Coverup', www.sourcewatch.org, 16 February 2008.

10 TVNZ One News, 'Timberlands PR Breached Rules', www.tvnz.co.nz, 12 May 2001.

11 IPG, 'Interpublic Group is Committed to Our Five Core Values', www.interpublic.com, accessed 25 April 2014.

12 But Bernays recoiled at the way manipulation and propagandizing was used for totalitarian ends. Hitler's propaganda minister, Joseph Goebbels, was reputed to prize Bernays' writings, a poignant irony given that Bernays was an Austrian-born Jew.

13 Sheldon Rampton and John Stauber, *Trust Us, We're Experts! How Industry Manipulates Science and Gambles With Your Future* (New York, 2001), p. 45.

14 'Front Groups', The Center for Media and Democracy, www.sourcewatch.org, 26 March 2013.

15 'Best Public Relations That Money Can Buy: A Guide to Food Industry Front Groups', Center for Food Safety, www.centerforfoodsafety.org, May 2013, p. 13.

16 'About EID', Energy in Depth, www.energyindepth.org, accessed 25 April 2014.

17 'About the International Food Information Council', IFIC, www.ific.us, 2011.

18 Center for Food Safety, 'Best Public Relations', p. 11.

19 'Policy Objectives of the Wise Use Movement', www.wildwilderness.org, accessed 24 April 2014.

20 James McCarthy, 'First World Political Ecology: Lessons from the Wise Use Movement', *Environment and Planning*, XXIV/7 (2002), pp. 1281–302; Sharon Beder, 'The Changing Face of Conservation: Commodification, Privatisation and the Free Market', in *Gaining Ground: In Pursuit of Ecological Sustainability*, ed. D. M. Lavingne (Guelph, 2006), pp. 83–97.

21 Center for Consumer Freedom, 'About Us: What is the Center for Consumer Freedom?' www.consumerfreedom.com, accessed 23 April 2014.

22 'Adbusters Overview', www.activistcash.com, accessed 23 April 2014.

23 Denise Deegan, *Managing Activism: A Guide to Dealing with Activists and Pressure Groups* (London, 2001); Keva Silversmith, *A PR Guide to Activist Groups* (2004).

24 Stephen Armstrong, 'The New Spies', *New Statesman* (7 August 2008).

25 Student/Farmworker Alliance, 'Busted, Part 2: Spy Scandal Linked to BK CEO!' www.sfalliance.org, 14 May 2008.

26 Amy Bennett, 'Burger King Fires Two for Posts About Farmworkers', *Fort Myers News Press* (14 May 2008); Eric Schlosser, 'Burger With Side of Spies', *New York Times* (7 May 2008).

27 Julie M. Rodriguez, 'Dow Chemical Pays Corporate Spies to Track Activist Group "The Yes Men"', www.care2.com, 29 February 2012; WikiLeaks, 'The Global Intelligence Files List of Documents. Release Stratford [sic] Monitored Bhopal Activists Including the Yes Men for Dow Chemical and Union Carbide', www.wikileaks.org, 27 February 2012.

28 Eamon Javers, *Broker, Trader, Lawyer, Spy: The Secret World of Corporate Espionage* (New York, 2010), p. x. See William Dinan and David Miller, eds, *Thinker, Faker, Spinner, Spy: Corporate PR and the Assault on Democracy* (London, 2007); also Paul Demko 'Corporate Spooks: Private Security Contractors Infiltrate Social Justice Organizations', UTN Reader (January–February 2009); Stephen Armstrong, 'The New Spies', *New Statesman* (7 August 2008).

29 John Stauber and Sheldon Rampton, 'MBD: Mission Despicable', *PR Watch*, second quarter, III/2 (1966).

30 John Elkington, 'Towards the Sustainable Corporation: Win-win-win Business Strategies for Sustainable Development', *California Management Review*, XXXVI/2 (1994), pp. 90–100.

31 Corporate Knights, 'The Global 100: World Leaders in Clean Capitalism', www.global100.org, accessed 25 April 2014.

32 'Our Code: It's What We Believe In', www.bp.com, accessed 25 April 2014.

33 'Ford Still Makes America's Worst Gas Guzzlers', www.publicmediacenter.org, accessed 25 April 2014.

34 'Making and Selling Responsibly', *Imperial Tobacco Annual Report and Accounts*, www.imperial-tobacco.com, 2011.

35 N. Jennifer Rosenberg and Michael Siegel, 'Use of Corporate Sponsorship as a Tobacco Marketing Tool: A Review of Tobacco Industry Sponsorship in the USA, 1995–99', *Tobacco Control*, X/3 (2001), pp. 239–46.

36 Shiv Malik, 'Arms Manufacturer Halts National Gallery Sponsorship after Protests', *The Guardian* (10 October 2012).

37 Lee Fang, 'Does the NRA Represent Gun Manufacturers or Gun Owners?', *The Nation* (14 December 2012).

38 Deborah Philips and Garry Whannel, *The Trojan Horse: The Growth of Commercial Sponsorship* (London, 2013).

39 Ian Roberts, 'Corporate Capture and Coca-Cola', *The Lancet*, CCCLXXII/9654 (2008), pp. 1934–5.

40 Slavoj Žižek, 'Nobody Has to be Vile', *London Review of Books*, XXVIII/7 (2006), p. 10.

41 'Corporate Responsibility: Community Investment', Katanga Mining Limited, www.katangamining.com, April 2014; Hannah Poole Hahn, Karen Hayes and Azra Kacapor, 'Breaking the Chain: Child Mining in the Democratic Republic of Congo', www.pactworld.org, October 2013.

6 Blame Government

1 OECD, *Government at a Glance* (Paris, 2013).

2 Georg Wenzelburger, 'Blame Avoidance, Electoral Punishment and the Perceptions of Risk', *Journal of European Social Policy*, XXIV/1 (2014), pp.80–91.

3 Christopher Hood, *Blame Game: Spin, Bureaucracy, and Self-preservation in Government* (Princeton, NJ, 2010).

4 Jon Kelly, 'The 10 Most Scandalous Euphemisms', *BBC News Magazine*, www.bbc.co.uk, 15 May 2013.

5 Denis Thompson, 'Moral Responsibility of Public Officials: The Problem of Many Hands', *American Political Science Review*, LXXIV (1980), pp. 905–16.

6 Robert Behn, *Rethinking Democratic Accountability* (Washington, DC, 2001), p. 3.

7 'ICM Europe Poll', www.theguardian.com, 2011.

8 Russell Dalton and Steven Weldon, 'Public Images of Political Parties: A Necessary Evil?' *West European Politics*, XXVIII/5 (2005), pp. 931–51.

7 I'm Sorry

1 Eshun Hamaguchi, 'A Contextual Model of the Japanese: Toward a Methodological Innovation in Japan Studies', *Journal of Japanese Studies*, XI/2 (1985), pp. 289–21.

2 '9TH LD: Hatoyama Quits Before Election, Hit by U.S. Base Fiasco', www.thefreelibrary.com, 2 June 2010.

3 See William Maddux, Peter Kim, Tesushi Okumura and Jeanne Brett, 'Cultural Differences in the Function and Meaning of Apologies, *International Negotiation*, XXVI/3 (2011), pp. 405–25.

4 Kim Willsher, 'John Galliano Sacked by Christian Dior Over Alleged Anti-Semitic Rant', *The Guardian* (1 March 2011); Lindsay Goldwert, 'John Galliano Anti-Semitic Rant Caught on Video; Slurs On Camera "I Love Hitler"', *New York Daily News* (28 February 2011).

5 'John Galliano Apologizes: "I Only Have Myself to Blame"', *Huffington Post* (3 February 2011).

6 Esther Addley, 'Disgraced Fashion Designer John Galliano Makes a Comeback', *The Guardian* (18 January 2013), p. 5.

7 Oliver Burkeman, 'Breaking Oprah's Rules: A Confession without Confessing', *The Guardian* (19 January 2013), p. 40.

8 Willy Brandt, *My Life in Politics* (London, 1992), p. 200.

9 Ibid., p. 200.

10 Joretta Purdue, '"Haunted" UM Pastor Reconciles with His Past', *United Methodist Review* (21 February 1997), p. 2.

11 Tom Bowman, 'Veteran's Admission to Napalm Victim a Lie: Minister Says He Never Meant to Deceive with "Story of Forgiveness"', *Sun National* (14 December 1997).

12 'Chris Huhne and Vicky Pryce Jailed: Judge's Sentencing Remarks in Full', *The Telegraph* (11 March 2013).

13 Ahan Kim, 'Lawmaker Backs Off Remark About Men Wearing Diapers on Their Heads', *Cox News Service*, ocssa.tripod.com, 21 September 2001.

14 'Drone Strikes Kill, Maim and Traumatize Too Many Civilians, U.S. Study Says', CNN Wire Staff, www.cnn.co.uk, 26 September 2012.

15 Reported by Zohar Kampf, 'Public (Non-) Apologies: The Discourse of Minimizing Responsibility', *Journal of Pragmatics*, XLI/11 (2009), p. 2261.

16 Ibid.

17 Michael Skapinker, 'The Sorry Business of Corporate Apologies', FT.com, 11 January 2010.

18 Guy Anker, 'Lloyds Says Sorry for Mis-selling', MoneySavingExpert.com, 14 June 2011.

19 'Full Transcript of PM's Speech', *The Australian*, 14 February 2008.

20 'Bloody Sunday: PM David Cameron's Full Statement', www.bbc.co.uk, 15 June 2010.

21 Rhoda Howard-Hassmann and Mark Gibney, 'Introduction: Apologies and the West', in *The Age of Apology: Facing Up to the Past*, ed. M. Gibney (Philadelphia, PA, 2008).

22 Anne Davies, 'Apology Was a Mistake, Says Feisty Howard', theage.com.au, 12 March 2008.

23 'If Armenian "Genocide" Proven, Turkey Will Apologize, Says Bagis', www.todayszaman.com, 2 April 2012.

24 'Statement by the Chief Cabinet Secretary Yohei Kono on the Result of the Study on the Issue of "Comfort Women"', Ministry of Foreign Affairs of Japan, www.mofa.go.jp, 3 August 1993.

25 Alasdair MacIntyre, *After Virtue: A Study in Moral Theory* (Bloomington, IN, 2007).

8 From Blame to Restoration

1 Abstracted from Janice Wearmouth, Rawry Mckinney and Tedd Glynn, 'Restorative Justice in Schools: A New Zealand Example', *Educational Research*, XLIX/1 (2007), pp. 37–49.

2 'Contemporaneous Record of a Restorative Justice Conference', www.why-me.org, October 2012.

3 Jung Jin Choi and Margaret Severson, '"What! What Kind of Apology is This?" The Nature of Apology in Victim Offender Mediation', *Children and Youth Services Review*, XXXI/7 (2009), p. 818.

4 Lawrence Sherman and Heather Strang, *Restorative Justice: The Evidence* (London, 2007).

5 'A Zero-tolerance School that Gave Pupils 717 Detentions in Three Days for Petty Offences was Slammed by Parents Yesterday', *Mirror News* (8 April 2011); 'Zero Tolerance: Pupils Put into "Isolation" For Wearing the "Wrong" Uniform to School', *Bournemouth Daily Echo* (6 September 2013).

6 Russell Skiba and Reece Peterson, 'The Dark Side of Zero Tolerance: Can Punishment Lead to Safe Schools?', *Phi Delta Kappan*, LXXX/5 (1999), pp. 372–82; Daniel Losen and Russell Skiba, 'Suspended Education', Southern Poverty Law Center, Montgomery, Alabama (2010), www.splcenter.org.

7 Deborah Fowler, Rebecca Lightsey, Janis Monger, Erica Terrazas and Lynn White, 'Texas's School-to-Prison Pipeline: Dropout to Incarceration', www.texasappleseed.net, October 2007.

8 Cecil Reynolds, Russell Skiba, Sandra Graham, Peter Sheras, Jane Conoley and Enedina Garcia-Vazquez, 'Are Zero Tolerance Policies Effective in the Schools? An Evidentiary Review and Recommendations', *American Psychologist*, LXIII/9 (2008), pp. 852–62; Lisa Cameron and Margaret Thorsborne, 'Restorative Justice and School Discipline: Mutually Exclusive?', in *Restorative Justice and Civil Society*, ed. H. Strang and J. Braithwaite (Cambridge, 2001).

9 See Jeremy Smith, 'Can Restorative Justice Keep Schools Safe?', www.greatergood.berkeley.edu, 6 March 2011.

10 All quotations are from 'National Evaluation of the Restorative Justice in Schools Programme', Youth Justice Board Publication (D61), Youth Justice Board for England and Wales, 2004.

11 David Karp and Beau Breslin, 'Restorative Justice in School Communities', *Youth and Society*, XXXIII/2 (2001), p. 270; Jeanne Stinchcomb, Gordon Bazemore and Nancy Riestenberg, 'Beyond Zero Tolerance: Restoring Justice in Secondary Schools', *Youth Violence and Juvenile Justice*, IV/2 (2006), pp. 123–47.

12 Susan Duncan, 'Workplace Bullying and the Role Restorative Practices Can Play in Preventing and Addressing the Problem', *Industrial Law Journal*, XXXII (2011), p. 2331.

13 Les Davey, 'Restorative Practices in Workplaces', www.restorativejustice.org.uk, 7 November 2010.

14 Simon Green, Gerry Johnstone and Craig Lambert, 'Reshaping the Field: Building Restorative Capital', *Restorative Justice*, I/3 (2013), pp. 305–25.

15 Ibid, p. 314.

16 Ibid, p. 317.

17 Ibid, p.318.

18 IPCC, 'IPPC Investigations: A Survey Seeking Feedback from Complainants and Police Personnel' (London 2009); Ade Adepitan, 'So Many Complaints, So Little Action: Do the Police Take Racism Seriously?', *The Guardian* (16 June 2014); Tamar Hopkins, 'An Effective System for Investigating Complaints Against the Police', Victoria Law Foundation (Melbourne, 2009).

19 Tim Prenzler, Mateja Mihinjac and Louise Porter, 'Reconciling Stakeholder Interests in Police Complaints and Discipline Systems', *Police Practice and Research*, XIV/2 (2013), pp. 55–168; Richard Young, Carolyne Hoyle, Karen Cooper and Roderick Hill, 'Informal Resolution of Complaints against the Police: A Quasi-experimental Test of Restorative Justice', *Criminal Justice*, V/3 (2005), pp. 279–317.

20 Madeline Fullard and Nicky Rousseau, 'Truth Telling, Identities, and Power in South Africa and Guatemala', International Center for Transnational Justice (New York, 2009); Jay Vora and Erika Vora, 'The Effectiveness of South Africa's Truth and Reconciliation Commission: Perceptions of Xhosa, Afrikaner, and English South Africans', *Journal of Black Studies*, xxxiv/3 (2004), pp. 301–22.

21 'The Voice of "Prime Evil"', www.news.bbc.co.uk, 28 October 1998.

22 Leigh Payne, *Unsettling Accounts: Neither Truth nor Reconciliation in Confessions of State Violence* (Durham, 2007), p. 265.

23 Zenon Szablowinski, 'Between Forgiveness and Unforgiveness', *Heythrop Journal*, li/3 (2010), p. 476.

24 Frederic Luskin, *Forgive for Good* (New York, 2010); Michael McCullough, Kenneth Pargament and Carl Thoresen, eds, *Forgiveness: Theory, Research, and Practice* (New York, 2000).

25 Jeanne Safer, *Forgiving and Not Forgiving: Why Sometimes it's Better Not to Forgive* (New York, 1999).

26 Jan-Heiner Tuck, 'Unforgivable Forgiveness? Jankelevitch, Derrida, and a Hope Against All Hope?', *Communio*, xxxi/4 (2004), p. 528.

Bibliography

1 Why Do We Blame?

Coates, D. Justin, and Neal Tognazzini, eds, *Blame: Its Nature and Norms* (Oxford, 2013)

Lamb, Sharon, *The Trouble with Blame* (Cambridge, MA, 1996)

Louie, Sam, *Asian Honor: Overcoming the Culture of Silence* (Bloomington, 2012)

Rapley, Robert, *Witch Hunts: From Salem to Guantanamo Bay* (Quebec, 2007)

2 Panics Old and New

Allen, Chris, *Islamophobia* (Farnham, 2010)

Critcher, Chas, *Moral Panics and the Media* (Berkshire, 2003)

Furedi, Frank, *Moral Crusades in an Age of Mistrust: The Jimmy Savile Scandal* (London, 2013)

Goode, Erich, and Nachman Ben-Yehuda, *Moral Panics: The Social Construction of Deviance* (London, 2009)

Wilson, John, and Boris Droždek, eds, *Broken Spirits: The Treatment of Traumatized Asylum Seekers, Refugees, War and Torture Victims* (London, 2004)

3 Blame Cultures

Dekker, Sidney, *Just Culture: Balancing Safety and Accountability* (Farnham, 2012)

Hood, Christopher, *The Blame Game: Spin, Bureaucracy, and Self-preservation in Government* (Princeton, 2010)

Power, Michael, *The Audit Society: Rituals of Verification* (Oxford, 1997)

Whittingham, Robert, *The Blame Machine: Why Human Error Causes Accidents* (London, 2004)

Williams, Kevin, 'State of Fear: Britain's "Compensation Culture" Reviewed', *Legal Studies*, xxv/3 (2005), pp. 499–514

4 Blaming the Organization

Alford, Fred, *Whistleblowers: Broken Lives and Organizational Power* (Ithaca, NY, 2001)

Jordan, Tim, *Activism: Direct Action, Hacktivism and the Future of Society* (London, 2002)

Klein, Naomi, *No Logo: Taking Aim at the Brand Bullies* (Toronto, 2000)

Lipman, Frederick, *Whistleblowers: Incentives, Disincentives and Protection Strategies* (New York, 2011)

Verso, ed., *We Are Everywhere – The Irresistible Rise of Global Anti-capitalism* (London, 2003)

5 The Empires Strike Back

Apollonio, Dorie, and Lisa Bero, The Creation of Industry Front Groups: The Tobacco Industry and "Get Government off Our Back"', *American Journal of Public Health*, xcvii/3 (2007), pp. 419–27

Banerjee, Bobby, *Corporate Social Responsibility: The Good, the Bad and the Ugly* (Northampton, MA, 2007)

Javers, Eamon, *Broker, Trader, Lawyer, Spy: The Secret World of Corporate Espionage* (New York, 2010)

Oliver, Sandra, *Public Relations Strategy* (London, 2009)

6 Blame Government

Bowles, Nigel, James Hamilton and David Levy, eds, *Transparency in Politics and the Media: Accountability and Open Government* (London, 2013)

Hood, Christopher, *Blame Game: Spin, Bureaucracy, and Self-preservation in Government* (Princeton, NJ, 2010)

Hughes, Andy, *A History of Political Scandals: Sex, Sleaze and Spin* (Barnsley, 2013)

Thompson, John, *Political Scandal: Power and Visibility in the Media Age* (Cambridge, 2000)

7 I'm Sorry

Kampf, Zohar, 'Public (Non-) Apologies: The Discourse of Minimizing Responsibility', *Journal of Pragmatics*, XLI/11 (2009), pp. 2257–70

Lind, Jennifer, *Sorry States: Apologies in International Politics* (New York, 2010)

Proeve, Michel, and Steven Tudor, *Remorse: Psychological and Jurisprudential Perspectives* (Farnham, 2010)

Smith, Nick, *I Was Wrong: The Meanings of Apologies* (Cambridge, 2008)

8 From Blame to Restoration

Bohm, Tomas, and Suzanne Kaplan, *Revenge: On the Dynamics of a Frightening Urge and its Taming* (London, 2011)

Rotberg, Robert, and Dennis Thompson, *Truth v. Justice: The Morality of Truth Commissions* (Princeton, NJ, 2010)

Safer, Jeanne, *Forgiving and Not Forgiving: Why Sometimes it's Better not to Forgive* (New York, 2000)

Strickland, Ruth, *Restorative Justice* (New York, 2004)

Acknowledgements

The book has benefited hugely from the constructive criticism and patience of Ben Hayes at Reaktion Books but, for any errors or omissions, the blame is truly mine.

Index